Mountain City

Mountain City

Gregory Martin

North Point Press

A division of Farrar, Straus and Giroux

New York

North Point Press
A division of Farrar, Straus and Giroux
19 Union Square West, New York 10003

Copyright © 2000 by Gregory Martin
All rights reserved
Distributed in Canada by Douglas & McIntyre Ltd.
Printed in the United States of America
Designed by Jonathan D. Lippincott
First edition, 2000

Library of Congress Cataloging-in-Publication Data
Martin, Gregory, 1971–
  Mountain City / Gregory Martin.
    p.   cm.
  ISBN 0-86547-594-6 (alk. paper)
  1. Mountain City (Nev.)—Social life and customs—20th century.   2.
Mountain City (Nev.)—Biography.   3. Martin, Gregory, 1971– .   4. Basque
Americans—Nevada—Mountain City—Biography.   I. Title.

F849.M68 M37 2000
979.3'16—dc21   99-056160

for Oliver and Anna

I am forever indebted to my mother and father, to the people of Mountain City, and especially to the Tremewan family, the Basañez family, the Graff family, and the Smiraldo family, who gave their stories and their lives to this book. Special thanks to Richard Shelton and Alison Deming, whose encouragement and advice helped make this book possible. Thanks to Dan Stolar, Jennifer Britz, Kyle Waide, and to Chris and Anna Martin, for their careful reading of early drafts. Thanks to Linda White at the University of Nevada Reno Basque Studies Program, for her help with the translations. Thanks also to Doug Stewart at Curtis Brown, and to Rebecca Saletan and Katrin Wilde at North Point Press. Finally, to my wife, Christine, for whose love, support, and razor-sharp editorial insight no acknowledgment of debt is sufficient.

Mountain City

My uncle Mel is telling a joke.

"This old Basco from Winnemucca got tired of herding sheep and decides to fly home to the Basque Country. He takes a seat on the plane, settles into it, and then a little before takeoff a stewardess comes over and says, 'Excuse me, sir, but this is first class. Your seat's back in row twenty-six.' But that Basco says, 'My name is-a Aitor Uberuaga, and I am-a going back to Bilbao. And I like-a this seat right here!'"

Mel's finger points down and pokes the checkout counter firmly, as if the store were the plane and the counter the seat in first class. Melvin Basañez is short, a little chubby, and has salt-and-pepper hair and a large, slightly hooked Basque nose. His accent now is that of his father, a man who at fourteen came from the Basque Country to northern Nevada to herd sheep. He came without speaking a word of English and in fifty years never learned to read or write. In fifty years he never once returned home.

"The stewardess doesn't know what to do, so she gets the copilot, who comes out and says to the Basco, 'Sir, I'm sorry, but this seat has been assigned to someone else. Your seat's back in row twenty-six. It's a fine seat.' Well that Basco's pretty steamed up by now. When they're off alone with all them sheep, they're not used to getting bossed around. So he says again, 'My name is-a Aitor Uberuaga, and I am-a going back to Bilbao. And I like-a this seat right here!' "

Mel's finger is this time pounding on the counter and his eyes are gleaming.

"So the stewardess and the copilot go back into the cockpit, and after a minute or two, here comes the captain. The captain leans over and says something to the Basco which the others can't make out, cause the captain's talking to him in confidence. Then, when the captain's done, the Basco nods his head, slaps the captain on the arm, and goes back and takes his seat in row twenty-six.

"Now this surprises that stewardess and copilot, and they ask the captain, 'What'd you say to him that made him change his mind?' And the captain says, 'Well, now, you got to know how to handle them Bascos. I told him that *this* section of the plane wasn't going to Bilbao.' "

The Frito-Lay man laughs, looking up from the jars of salsas and dips he's been stocking. Gramps and I shake our heads, trying not to grin, and my aunt Lou turns back to the produce case from the aisle where she was standing, listening. And for a short while Tremewan's Store rests suspended in the atmosphere of the joke, the same joke Mel told Jerry, the UPS man, the day before, and Bert, the school bus driver, the day before that. It's eight-thirty in the morning in December, and no customers

4

have yet arrived. The soda pop case hums. Outside the two wide front windows, in the store's reflected light, magpies gather on the opposite shoulder of the highway where earlier Gramps scattered the day-old popcorn. The ignition of the Frito-Lay truck catches, its diesel engine turns over in the cold, and the magpies startle into the predawn dark. Inside, Mel, Gramps, and I haven't moved from our spots by the front counters, and Lou is the only one working at something, but leisurely, picking out the tired grapes and placing them in the pocket of her green apron.

Mel turns to me, grinning, and says, "Did you catch the new wrinkle?"

I hadn't, but I was going over the joke again in my head because I knew Mel would ask.

"I thought her up back in the deep freeze this morning: 'Well, now, you got to know how to handle them Bascos.' That line of the captain's, that's a new one. I think it improves the story quite a bit."

My uncle Mel has a Basco joke for nearly every occasion, and he tells them so often that they become highly refined. The store's five cramped, overcrowded aisles are decorated with evidence of his sense of humor. Mounted on a wall above a rack of bright orange clothes is a camouflage cap with a set of antlers growing out its top: BASCO HUNTING HAT. Hanging from a hook next to a few gardening tools is a plastic bag full of Cheerios: BASCO DONUT SEEDS. On another hook above the bread and pastries, the looped plastic off a six-pack of beer is stapled to the end of a wooden ruler: BASCO FLYSWATTER.

The Basco never makes out too well in these jokes. In a culture where much of the humor relies on a more familiar race or ethnic group for the butt of its jokes, and in a culture where these jokes are almost always told by someone from outside that group, the Bascos provide their own butts for their own jokes. Case in point: Lou recently won a horse trailer in a 4-H raffle. Lou and Mel don't own any horses and neither has ever been a rancher. Lou just thought she'd enter to support the 4-H. When Lou found out she'd won, the first thing she said was, "Well, I don't have a horse, but I got part of one."

In response to this, Mel later said, "You know, it's not clear what she meant by that. She could have been talking about either a part of her or all of me."

Lou smiled and said nothing, which made it more clear.

Mountain City is one mile long, limit to limit. Birch and golden willow shade the yards and porches of low framed houses and trailer homes, and rusted chain-link fences separate lawn from sage. In the meadow below town, the east fork of the Owyhee meanders north, past willows and ryegrass and fence posts and wire, and above everything, like a low, uneven wall, rounded hills rise up and circle the town, obscuring the view of higher mountains.

At the north end of town is Mountain City's "commercial district." Seven buildings. The Forest Service building, the post office, and the Steakhouse on the west side of the highway, closest to the river. On the east side, the Chambers' Motel, the Miner's Club, Reed's Service Station, and Tremewan's Store.

Highway 225 is Mountain City's Main Street, but no one calls it that. As it enters town, the highway slows and becomes Davidson Street, after a man who used to run a mining store in town before the turn of the century, before the bust and abandonment. The name is posted on a few white wooden signs, but no one uses that name either. People call it "the highway" or "the road." There are no stoplights and no stop signs. Eighty-four miles south, the highway ends in Elko, and there are no towns in between. North from Mountain City, it's four miles to the Duck Valley Indian Reservation, thirteen miles to Owyhee, the only town on the reservation, and sixteen miles to Idaho, where the road becomes Highway 51.

Thirty-three people live in Mountain City. I come and go, but when I'm here that makes thirty-four.

I was ten when Gramps first took me to Rio Tinto. I knew the Rio Tinto was somewhere up in the mountains behind Mountain City, and Gramps had once lived and worked at the mine there, and now it was a ghost town. But I had never been there before, and one summer afternoon when business was slow at Tremewan's, I asked Gramps what was up there at the Rio Tinto. And he said, "Let's go."

We went outside and walked the quarter mile up the highway to my grandparents' place and the garage Gramps had built beside it. We climbed into his old, brown Ford pickup and drove south out of town past the 101 Ranch, where meadow paralleled the road on both sides. The windows were down, and the smell of wet sage rushed in. It had rained that morning, and the storm still gathered on the mountains around us, and the meadow's green darkened or shined as the outlined clouds changed directions.

We crossed the Owyhee outside town and Gramps took his foot off the accelerator and the pickup coasted. "A sandhill crane," he said, nodding, and I followed his eyes out the windshield and across the meadow. It stood gray and white in shadow at the edge of the river in the willows, and if Gramps hadn't said something I wouldn't have seen it.

We turned west off the highway onto a gravel road that wound steeply up the side of a mountain. A rock-strewn gully ran intermittently beside and below us, and Gramps shifted into a lower gear and the pickup labored up the grade. The gully deepened, and stands of aspen rose up where pools formed and moss grew on rocks, and I thought of how I was never lonely with Gramps though he rarely spoke. I thought of how loneliness had nothing to do with quiet.

"Some of your great-granddad's carvings are down in them trees," Gramps said. He meant Grandma's dad, not his, and he stopped the truck and I got out and scrambled down into the aspen grove, where the soft light was softer still. Grandma called her dad *Aíta,* and he was a Basco and a sheepherder and had owned a hotel, and he'd died long before I was born. All around were carvings in the bark, like black ink on parchment, and the words had swelled as the trees had swelled but I could see that one tree said *Euskadi* and on another a stick man I knew wore a beret. A thin, rusted horseshoe hung from a bent nail. An ash pan had become a part of the leaves and flattened ground. I looked for the names Domingo and Zabala, like I'd seen other places, but I couldn't find them, and I wondered if Aíta had been lonely here, and that was hard for me to imagine.

We drove on. The gully turned south and the road went on alone, skirting the mountainside. Then the road leveled, and we looked out on a broad plateau. Gramps parked the truck in the road, and we got out and walked. He was not yet seventy then, and to me, at ten, he seemed nearly as able and fit as any man at any age. He had not followed me down into the aspen grove, but I had looked back because I thought he might. We walked down the road and before long reached the first foundation. An outline of crumbling cement. A depression in the earth. Rebar grew from the foot-high walls, securing nothing but sky. We stopped and I walked around and inside. Gramps had his hands in his pockets and he whistled some. I found a pair of eyeglasses, the glass gone. The frames had shriveled somehow and wouldn't have fit an infant's face. I gave them to Gramps, and he turned them over in his splotched hands and gave them back to me. We walked past row after row of foundations. Rusted-out cars and trucks and stoves declined into the soil, the flaked oxidized-orange steel like a perpetual metal autumn.

I didn't swing on the swings or slide down the slide in the overgrown playground, though I could have. I didn't want to. The schoolhouse was two stories high. Its walls were concrete, the only walls left standing anywhere on that windblown plateau. The roof had been blown or torn off, the doors were all gone, and the ceiling of the first story and the floor of the second were missing also, so that inside I looked up and saw the gray sky penciled with rain.

We walked across a field, away from the school and the foundations. Thick metal cables lay randomly on the ground and in places the rocky earth had been stained purple. At the edge of the field there was a hole the size of a mountain turned inside out. Dark machinery that had extracted ore stood on ledges at different distances down in the hole, and there was a wooden tower on a ledge, and the wood was dark also, like tar. Beyond the hole, in the distance, was Mountain City, laid out below us like an aerial photograph, and something about this view lent the place a sense of design, of symmetry and stability that I had at that moment first begun to question.

From up there I could look down and make out every place. I put names to the inhabited places, and I could see the river and the meadow. I could see the metal roof of Tremewan's Store, and I said so. Gramps nodded. He didn't point out any of these things because I could see them for myself, and because I didn't ask. I didn't ask the questions I would later ask about the Rio Tinto, questions he has since answered, because those questions didn't occur to me then: *What did you do here? Why did everyone leave? Were you sad to go?* And Gramps didn't turn to me and say that it was still beautiful, that things now were no better or worse than things then. Whatever thoughts he had he didn't share, and I didn't know how to ask him to do that, like I do now, sometimes.

The wind was blowing. It was getting colder, and it began to rain. Neither of us had a jacket. We both still wore our green aprons from Tremewan's Store, and Gramps said, "Are you cold?"

"I don't care about the cold," I said.

"Neither do I," he said.

My grandmother's maiden name is Anastasia Zabala. She isn't quite five feet tall. *Zabala,* in Basque, means "wide," and there's no better way to describe Grandma than this.

Grandma and I speak to each other each day in Basque. We speak only in simple phrases because that's all the Basque I know. *Apurbat.* A little. My mom never learned Basque. Neither did my aunts Lou or Di or Sarah. None of my cousins knows Basque. But I've started asking, and Grandma has been teaching me.

We greet each other each morning.

Egun on, Amama.

Egun on, Gregorio.

In the evenings, long after Gramps has gone to bed at eight, and before I walk outside into the night air and climb the steps to apartment three,

Gabon, Amama.
Gabon, Gregorio.
She's sitting at the kitchen table reading, or quilting, or we've been talking, and she's been holding my hand, patting it, squeezing it, telling me stories.

Then Aita would send all us kids around to the saloons and shops and rooming houses to gather up all the Bascos and bring them back to the hotel. There were eight of us, so we could usually get most of the ones in town, and some we'd have to lead back by the hand because you know. Then all them Bascos would show at the Overland in their funeral clothes and Aita would herd 'em into the recyvydor and the deceased would be laid out in a suit in a casket in the middle of the room. (Aita kept the suit and the casket in the closet.) We might have fifty Bascos corralled in there. Ama would say a prayer and we'd all bow our heads and Aita would take a picture of everyone gathered around the open casket looking serious, the men with their hands behind their backs, the women fingering rosaries. And not long after, everybody'd go back to where they were before. Aita would send the photograph and a note to the family back in the old country. And he always said to Ama, There is no poor Bascos in America. *She would just look at him. And I would ask,* Why did that old sheepman die? *And Aita would say,* Homesickness.

Grandma learned to speak English at the kindergarten in Elko. But before that, she learned some phrases from her older brothers Frank and Pete and Raymond.

---

*One day I got so mad at that darned cat cause he kept batting the altar
cloth me and Ayah were sewing for the mass in the recyvydor, and so I
stood up and said,* I am going to throw this window out that cat.
*And Ayah didn't know better either because we were twins so she was
little too, but Frank and Pete knew better and I never to this day lived it
down and that's been eighty years.*

In 1913 Grandma was born in the Overland Hotel, in a special
room on the first floor. All the Zabala children were born in that
room, as were most Bascos in Elko in those years. When my great-
grandmother wasn't giving birth herself, she was the midwife.

*The boys would be outside playing and Ayah and Lenore and Aug and
me would have to stay inside with Ama sewing altar cloths and doing
laundry and changing linens and cleaning chamber pots and cooking and
that's just how it was back then. And Pete got to go to Reno to college,
and Frank went to Notre Dame until Aita lost the Overland to the
Depression. So none of us girls got to go to college even if Aita would
have let us. And Frank said he was the first Basco to go to Notre Dame,
and nobody knew what a Basco was and he wasn't joking, and Frank
has been gone a long, long time.*

When my mom and her sisters were all teenagers, they stood on
the corner in front of the Commercial Hotel in Elko and

watched as the Overland Hotel was torn to the ground. A few others stood with them. A couple of old Bascos. Some people just passing by. Grandma was working down the street at J. M. Capriola's. She wouldn't come out and watch.

Sometimes Ayah and me would creak open those glass doors and sneak into the recyvydor. If we'd been caught, if Ama or Aita ever found us playing in there, I don't even want to think about what would have happened. But they never did. And the boys would be outside playing in the afternoon, or it was after dinner on Saturday and a dance was in the dining room and we could hear the music and all the Bascos laughing but it was quiet in the recyvydor. And we'd go in there and sneak around, and we always felt the old world in the recyvydor, with the candles and the altar and Mary and the baby Jesus, and sometimes we'd make ourselves cry the way Ama would cry in there alone, and we were very mysterious.

Now, whenever some old Basco comes into the store, Grandma introduces me as her "Basco grandson." I usually make it through the first exchange:

> *Zer moduz?*
> *Ondo, Ta zu?*
> *Ondo.*

But after that the look on my face gives me away. The words come too fast.

Then everything slows down. An old man in a red beret takes me firmly by the arm, mouths out each word. He's barrel-chested, strong, and I imagine him, younger, hefting a great granite boulder before a crowd in a cobbled courtyard somewhere. He says, very slowly, *Eskerrik asko. Thank you.* Another time, Grandma's kindergarten classmate Ada Eguiren takes a pen from my apron, writes on my palm. *Etorri. Come.* She looks at me. *Come see me,* she says. She nods at Grandma, her eyebrows raised. *Bai,* Grandma says. *We will come.* Then I repeat the new words slowly, several times, until everyone is satisfied. Mel tinkers with my pronunciation. Grandma is smiling. "He is learning," she says. *Gero arte,* I say, as they leave. *Until next time.*

Only a few people who shop regularly at Tremewan's Store pay at each purchase; that includes residents in town, the area's ranchers and miners, and the Indians from the Duck Valley Reservation. Customers keep a copy of their receipt, the store keeps a copy stapled in a book under the customer's name, and then most customers pay their bill at the end of each month. Some people, like the Thompsons and the Donnelsons, pay once a year in the fall, after they've sold off their cows.

The store doesn't accept credit cards—only cash, check, or Tremewan's Store credit. One older woman in town writes rubber checks for all her groceries. After she's gone, one of us takes the check from the till and staples it and the receipt to her page in the credit book. At the end of the month, Lou totals the checks and mails the receipts and a bill to the woman's sister in Reno. The sister pays the bill, and the process begins again. I don't know how long this has gone on. When she writes her checks, neither party to the transaction suggests by any comment or gesture that things are not entirely as they seem.

About fifteen years ago, after trouble over how much a few people owed, the store began requiring a signature on the credit slip. That way, there was a verifiable record of who bought what and when.

I turned thirteen that summer, and Lou and Mel agreed to let me run the cash registers (I had only stocked shelves and bagged groceries before), and so I became familiar with the store's idiosyncratic credit system. No one told me not to ask certain people to sign their slip.

Rosella Chambers is the oldest woman in Mountain City. She's ninety-one, and so thin a gust of wind could send her tumbling with the tumbleweeds. She has lived in Mountain City for sixty years and has been shopping at the store since it became a store. She remembers back when the floor of the store was just a platform built for a dance on the Fourth of July.

One day that summer, I asked Rosella if she would please sign her name at the bottom of her credit slip.

"Young man, I've been coming in here since before you were born, since before any of you came into this country, and I have never once signed my name for nothing. Do you think I'm about to skip town *now*, run out on my bill *now*, after all these years? Where am I going to go? Where?"

I was stunned by Rosella's outburst, but I intended to keep my position up front at the registers. I held my ground.

"I'm sorry, Rosella, but it's policy."

With great aplomb, I extended the credit slip toward her on the counter, took my pen from my apron pocket, and, resolved, set it down next to the slip.

"Well I never." She seized the pen and with two bold strokes that nearly rent the slip to pieces, she wrote an X. A very large X. She snatched her bag of groceries and marched out the door.

Rosella informed me later that she'd been testing me, and I had passed. To this day, wherever I am, I receive a Christmas card signed both in the return address and at the end with an X.

Every morning at ten, the widows of Mountain City meet at the Miner's Club to drink coffee and play the slots. We call them the widows because that's what they call themselves. There are four of them: Rosella Chambers, Bobbie Culley, Margaret Hall, and Dorothy Ratliff. All are over seventy, all have gray or white hair and the tightly curled perms expected of widows, and all have lived in Mountain City for years and years.

The Miner's Club is the only bar in town. A dilapidated wood building with a classic western façade, it shares its south wall with Tremewan's Store, a circumstance Mel refers to as "a Siamese arrangement." Through the wall, the widows at their slots can hear clearly Mel's baritone renditions of "Hey, Good Lookin'" and "Makin' Whoopee," which he dedicates to them when he's over by the wall stocking soups, and likewise Lou, stocking produce, can tell when Margaret has hit the jackpot by the clinking of coins and her pious exclamation, "My God in heaven!"

At ten, the widows meet Eddie, the owner and daytime bar-tender, at the bar's front door to open the place for business.

Eddie is a small, thin man in his fifties with bad teeth and a jaundiced complexion. He unlocks the door, and they all go in together. A jukebox waits quietly just inside the door. Eight booths with cracked and duct-taped red vinyl seats extend along the wall across from a long, wooden bar. A pool table sits at the far end of the room. The table's green felt surface is perfectly level, but the tile floor slopes away beneath it like a boat ramp, making the game a bit more challenging.

Eddie puts on coffee, and the widows assume their places at the slot machines. Sometimes they play video poker. (There's only one machine, so they take turns.) They sit on chrome-legged stools beneath the rows of hard hats which line the walls. There are at least a hundred hard hats. Eddie has collected them from different mines all over Nevada. Hand-painted on the back of each hard hat in Eddie's relatively steady hand is the name of the mine it came from and, if known, the name of the miner and a date. Some date back to the nineteenth century. Some date back a few years. All the mines named on the hard hats went bust. A hard hat from the last mine to support Mountain City is on the wall. EDDIE BARNES   RIO TINTO   1947. Like many artists, Eddie won't put up an explanatory sign or give a talk on the exhibit's significance.

Beneath the hard hats, the widows drink their coffee, slide their coins down the throats of the machines, and leisurely pull their respective handles. They are experts. They talk a little and tease Eddie, who is always grumpy in the mornings and who has usually by then cracked open his first beer.

The widows have only one rule for membership, and they apply it strictly and without exception. You must be a widow. Merely being old or gray or frail or lonely or divorced, singly or in combination, is not enough. Your husband must be dead.

My grandma is eighty-four and has gray hair and a tightly curled perm and has lived in Mountain City for forty years, but she doesn't qualify. She won't admit it, but this is a source of great frustration for her. And lost irony. Grandma doesn't really want to be a widow, but she doesn't want to be excluded either. But the widows won't have her. Not until Gramps gives up the ghost.

Although Grandma sees the widows in the store almost every day, and sees them once a week at the meetings of the Mountain City Quilting Society, and once a week at the meetings of the Mountain City Homemakers Club, she's bitter about their mornings at the Miner's Club.

Each morning at ten, from our places at the registers, we see out the front windows Bobbie and Margaret and Dorothy walking down the highway past the store. Rosella lives up on the hill by the old schoolhouse, and we see her pull up in her old blue Jeep. The widows see us too, and they wave pleasantly. If Grandma is in the store at this time and sees them coming, she heads for the back. She won't wave to the widows.

An old Basco couple from Boise stops in Tremewan's Store on their way down to Las Vegas to see a show. Mel, of course, knows them. He chats with them awhile, and then as they're leaving, he shouts after them, *"Ondo ibili eta gutxi gastatu!"* This translates to "Have a good time, but don't spend all your money!"

It's an old sheepherder expression, one that Mel heard all the time growing up in the Martin Hotel in Winnemucca, a Basque hotel where his mother worked as a chambermaid and waitress. The expression was something one Basco would say to another Basco who was headed out on the town. While many Basque sheepherders were known for their frugality, for all the money they sent back to the old country, and for the large bands of sheep they came to own over the years, others were notorious for their startling lack of economic sense. They would spend nine months out on the range with the sheep, the whole time fighting off going crazy from loneliness. *Sheeped,* they called it. *Sagebrushed.* In November, when the lambs were shipped and two summer bands were consolidated into a single winter one, half an outfit's herders would get laid off until March, until lambing. These Bascos would come into town, to the Basque hotels, and drink and dance and gamble at the casinos and shop at the "girls stores," and they'd lose all they'd earned the previous year in a matter of days or weeks.

Mel's dad married late, when he was over forty, and his old single ways died hard. Even after he quit sheepherding, went to work for the railroad, and lived year-round at home with Mel and Mel's mom in Winnemucca, he wasn't always around in the evenings. He was out spending their money.

Mel's Basco expression is one of so many pithy expressions in the West, in northern Nevada, which capture and contain an entire context, an entire immigrant world. Like so many expressions of this kind, its context is gone, extinct, or so near extinct it's irrevocable. But Mel's still putting the expression to use. He can't help thinking it, context or no context.

Mel was the president of his senior class at Elko High School, but he didn't go to college. His parents didn't encourage him to go. He was raised by and beside immigrant Basques who had little or no command of English and who, by necessity, valued physical work far more than education. They had no education. Mel grew up knowing what it meant to swing a shovel or load a railcar or walk behind a band of sheep until the light had left the sky. He knew what it meant to empty and clean chamber pots, change thousands of linens, and wait tables at breakfast, lunch, and dinner. He hadn't done much of those things, but he knew what they meant. From his earliest memories, he'd witnessed the weariness in his parents and in the men and women who joined them at the long table in the dining room of the Martin Hotel.

After high school, Mel drove a laundry truck for two years, delivering dry cleaning all over northern Nevada. He drove more than four hundred miles a day. He'd grown up knowing about weariness, and he hadn't escaped it. Shortly after he and Lou were married, Grandma and Gramps offered them part ownership of Tremewan's Store if they would come to Mountain City and help run it, seven days a week, ten hours a day, 362 days a year. Mel quit driving the laundry truck the next day. Mel considered it a privilege to be able to talk to customers and once in a while sit on the store's front counter and read a magazine or the newspaper. He considered himself lucky.

Mel had seen my mother go through college, and he'd seen what an education had done for her. She'd become a college professor. Mel and Lou and Grandma and Gramps all helped pay her way through school. Back then, Mel always asked my mother what she'd learned so far. During her summers home from college, when she wore the green apron and worked in the store, she explained to him the principles of economics, and he picked them up quickly and applied them to his own work each day. Mel took great pride in my mother's education.

But the course of my education puzzled Mel deeply.

"Let's hear some more of that philosophy," he said, one slow summer afternoon. During my summers off from college in Virginia, I, too, went to Mountain City and put on the green apron. Every day of those summers, and sometimes more than once each day, Mel asked me to share with him something I'd learned "back east." He always approached the subjects of my schooling devilishly, obnoxiously, and he always tried to test my new knowledge, to shake it up some and see if it held water.

"There's this Greek philosopher who lived back around the time of Plato and Socrates."

"Those same guys we talked about the other day," Mel added.

"That's right."

"I've been thinking about those guys, and how you were saying their time in history was one of the greatest times."

"One of the greatest periods of thought in all of Western culture," I said importantly.

"I remember you saying that," Mel said. "But what I can't figure is the sexuality. I've been thinking about this. These days, when we see one of them priests messing with the young altar boys, we condemn it and rightly so. Now if that's the arrangement they had back then, and it was smiled on, then I can't figure what's so great about them or that time."

"That's not the reason it was considered great. It was considered great for the quality of thinking."

"How can you separate the two?"

"Let me get to what I was saying."

"Let's hear her."

"There was this Greek philosopher named Zeno of Elea, and he came up with this paradox."

"The man's name was *Zeno*."

"That's right."

"They sure had some strange names back then."

"And Melvin Basañez isn't a strange name?"

"You've got a point," Mel said, satisfied, grinning. He loved interrupting me like this.

I told Mel that Zeno believed he could prove that motion was an illusion. I told him that, according to Zeno, he could never reach any destination, because he always had to go halfway first. And when he got halfway, then from there, he'd have to go halfway again. And so on. Eventually he'd be taking such small steps that he wouldn't really be going anywhere.

"Let me see if I got this right," Mel said, a bit agitated. "Is this Zeno saying I can't walk across the street to that old service station because I have to go to the middle of the highway first? And once I get there, I have to go to the road shoulder? Is that the thinking?" Mel was looking out the front window, pointing.

"You've got it."

"Son, I didn't just fall off the turnip truck. I'll bet you this store I can walk over and put my hand on the green door of that garage. And when I get there I'll wave to you. And then I'll come back here and shake your hand. How does that sound? I'll even do it by this guy Zeno's method. It might take me a couple three hours to do her, but I'll bet I can."

"I know," I said. "It's a paradox. On paper Zeno sounds pretty good, but in practice, you can prove him wrong."

"Lots of things sound good on paper," Mel said flatly. And then he thought for a moment and added, "These Greeks are supposed to be some of the best thinkers ever?"

"That's what they say."

"Let me ask you another question."

"Shoot."

"When you were back east there, did they ever teach you one thing you could use?"

For days afterwards, Mel brought up Zeno of Elea to almost everyone who came in the store.

"Listen to what my nephew picked up back east," he'd say. "See if you think this will ever help him get a job."

"That won't even get him a job haying," Jim Connolley said, after he'd heard Mel's version of the paradox. "Not for me. I've got no time for philosophy. Sounds to me like an excuse to do a half-ass job."

"If you're going to Wendover," Mel said, "don't stop in Wells."

Wells is the town halfway between Elko and Wendover as you travel east on I-80, toward the Nevada–Utah state line, and Mel's expression was one used around northern Nevada to mean, essentially, "If you start something, finish it." Though the meaning of the expression had virtually nothing to do with the paradox, Mel began including it in his version of the story, as if it was something he would say to Zeno if he ever got the opportunity. "Zeno says you can only go halfway, but I say, 'If you're going to Wendover, don't stop in Wells.'"

Mel never truly appreciated the theoretical power of the paradox until he heard Rosella's interpretation. She'd come in the store one morning after her session of coffee and slots with Dorothy and Margaret and Bobbie. She was in no hurry, and Mel told her about Zeno and his problem.

"What if you *say* you're going to Wendover, but you really

mean to go to Wells," Rosella argued. "Then, halfway to Wendover, you're where you want to be."

Mel thought that Rosella's take on the paradox was the best
he'd heard, and before long he stopped referring to the paradox
as something his nephew had learned "back east." He'd say,
"Have you heard the one about Zeno from Elea?"

Whenever I make the long drive to Mountain City, Grandma waits up for me, sitting at the kitchen table reading or writing letters. Eleven. Midnight. Two in the morning. She thinks it's nice to have someone to talk to after a long night of driving, and it is. She's baked cookies and has a glass of milk in the refrigerator. The bed is made in apartment three, the apartment often left vacant for family, and the rooms are vacuumed and clean. We talk, and I unwind, and she fills me in on each of Mountain City's residents and our relatives living all over Elko County, many of whom I've never met. After an hour or so, I give her a hug and go to bed. In the morning, we all eat breakfast together, and then I walk down to the store with Gramps.

My grandparents' place sits on a flat rise at the south end of town. The front of the building looks out on the highway, and the back holds the view of the meadow and the river. The two-

story building is painted white with green trim, and at each of
its corners an outdoor staircase leads up to a furnished, one-
bedroom apartment. A weathered wooden sign planted in the
grass in front says, in faded red, hand-painted letters, APART-
MENTS FOR RENT. My grandparents live on the ground floor
and rent out the four upstairs apartments to the area's miners and
ranch hands.

Structurally, it's a rickety affair, held together more by stub-
bornness and will than by nails or any other building material. In
a good windstorm, the old wood walls give and creak, and in
winter, the flat copper roof, overburdened with snow, sags
deeply, and as the days grow warmer and the temperature rises,
it leaks. By spring, ceiling tiles in all four upstairs apartments are
swollen and trickling and threatening flood, and then my grandparents supply the miners and ranch hands with buckets and
help them rearrange the furniture curiously about their rooms.

Gramps and his dad built the apartment building in 1937, but
they didn't build it for themselves, and they didn't build it in
Mountain City. They built it up at the Rio Tinto mine, as hous-
ing for miners and their families.

The Rio Tinto had boomed in 1934, and after a year of producing copper at a steady profit, the owners decided to build a
"model community." They built offices and houses and apartment buildings, a hospital, a grammar school, a high school with
a gymnasium, track, and athletic field. They built a movie house,
a community center, a commissary, a newspaper plant, and a
sawmill. They uprooted scrub brush and sage and planted grass
for yards and trees to line the main street.

Gramps and his dad hired on at the Rio Tinto in 1936. Before that, they'd worked together at odd jobs since they lost their ranch in the Depression six years earlier. In good weather, they broke saddle horses and hired out to ranchers when there was work. They built roads and fence for the Forest Service. They dug graves for the mortuary in Elko and flagged down trains as brakemen for the Western Pacific. In winter, they set pins in the bowling alley in Elko for three cents a line. They set one hundred lines a day. With each pin at five pounds, and with ten pins a line, they lifted five thousand pounds a day—from their knees. One winter, they went to Carlin to cut ice for Pacific Fruit. From manmade ponds dug out beside the railroad tracks, they sawed blocks of ice, shaved them smooth with scrapers, sent them up a conveyor belt, and loaded them into insulated refrigerator cars on trains headed back east.

For Gramps and his dad, the dream of the West never meant what Louis L'Amour or Hollywood said and continued to say it meant, over and over and over. They never thought they were living out a horse opera. They took the jobs that were available, because they didn't want to go someplace else. They were trying to figure a way to stick to the landscape, with whatever glue was handy.

At Rio Tinto they hired on as carpenters, living in a tent through the first winter. Gramps and Grandma had been married the previous fall, and in the spring she joined them there.

In its heyday, fifteen hundred people lived at Rio Tinto, and the mine employed three hundred miners in three eight-hour shifts. It became the largest producer of copper in Elko County's history. On January 18, 1938, the town printed its first newspaper, the *Rio Tinto News*. A social was planned for the town's youth. The sewing club was to meet, a club to which my grand-mother belonged. That Saturday night an apron and overall dance was scheduled. On Sunday, the town's baseball team was to play Winnemucca. Joel McCrea starred in *Woman Chases Man,* and next week's movie was *Mountain Music* with Bob Burns and Martha Raye.

When the owners had built everything they set out to build, they offered the carpenters jobs in the mines, and many took them. Gramps and his dad did not. It wasn't that they wanted to leave Rio Tinto. The work had been steady for two years and the pay was good. And both men loved this part of northeastern Nevada. The Tremewan Ranch had been only twenty miles to the south, on the other side of the canyon. But they would not stay. They would not go underground. The list of Tremewans dead from black lung was too long.

In 1869, the Tremewans came to Nevada from Cornwall, where they'd worked in tin mines beneath the ocean's floor. Cornishmen were renowned for their skill underground, and all over the West they were imported to work in the mines. People called them Cousin Jacks. "Cousins" because of their close-knit communities within the ethnic amalgamation that was the West, and "Jacks" because of their skill with single- and double-jack drills.

Both Gramps's grandfather and great-grandfather had died young from miner's consumption. Gramps and his dad had vowed that they would not. All men die, but they didn't have to die like that, their lungs filled with ashen fluid, drowning in an arid land. They went back to Elko to work for the railroad.

The Rio Tinto went bust in September of 1947, and within a year the place was a ghost town. Even the trees were uprooted and replanted elsewhere. In the spring of 1948, after all the houses were long gone, the apartment buildings up at the Rio Tinto were cut in three pieces and hauled in sections down the mountain on long flatbed trucks. Four of the five buildings were pieced back together in Carlin, Battle Mountain, Winnemucca, and Wells.

In the fall of 1958, after buying the store that would become Tremewan's Store and moving from Elko to Mountain City, Grandma and Gramps bought the apartment building on the flat rise at the south end of town, a building Gramps and his dad had built two miles away and two decades before.

The fact that Mel and Lou Basañez run Tremewan's Store puzzles some people, especially newcomers. After Grandma and Gramps retired, Mel and Lou became full owners, and they decided to keep the store's name the same. No need to confuse people, they figured.

Since then, shipping orders and invoices from Associated Food and Bonanza Produce and Budweiser and Coca-Cola arrive in the mail addressed to Melvin and Louise Tremewan. When the phone rings and the caller asks for Melvin Tremewan, Mel usually says something like, "Yes, this is Melvin Basañez of Tremewan's Store."

"I'm sorry," the caller says, "I'm looking for Melvin Tremewan."

"You're not getting me here," Mel says, agitated. "There is no

Melvin Tremewan. I'm the guy you want to talk to. There's no other Melvin for a hundred miles."

"I've got the invoice right here in my hand, sir, and it says, clearly, Melvin Tremewan."

Then Mel gives in. "Okay. You got me. I'm Melvin Tremewan. What can I help you with?"

After such conversations, Mel looks drained, defeated, as if the entire grocery world has conspired against him. Often, Gramps is sitting right there, enjoying the whole thing.

Mel says to him, "For thirty-five years I've been called Melvin Tremewan. Just once, I wish someone would come in here and say, 'I'm looking for Oliver Basañez. Is he around?' And then before anybody gets a chance to say anything different, I'm going to say, 'You bet he is. He's the old-timer right over there, sitting on the counter.' What do you think of that?"

"I may have married a Basco," Gramps says, "but I'm a far cry from ever becoming one."

In order to confuse people further, Mel sometimes calls Tremewan's Store "Melbertson's." He employs supermarket lingo. "Glazed donuts are over in bakery," he says, or "You'll find that back in dairy," or "Let me ask the manager of our produce department." He cups his hands over his mouth and, in a loud, muffled voice, he imitates an intercom: "Louise, Louise, price check on aisle twenty-nine, Louise." He subjects customers to the same treatment: "Coleen James, Coleen James, come to the butcher's counter please, Coleen James. Your children are playing with the meat slicer." Coleen James, a Paiute woman who runs the Head Start program in Owyhee, is standing in front of the cereals, considering her options. Mel can see the top of her head above the Cheerios. Her children are hiding behind the meat counter, playing along.

In 1961, Gramps built the barnlike garage which sits beside the apartments. He was hoping to block the wind a bit, slow it down some before it reached his place. Besides that, he figured it would be nice to have somewhere to park his pickup and keep his shop. But those were secondary considerations. The wind was the thing. It was ruthless. Came right through the house, through your skin, into your bones.

Gramps's workbench stretches across the entire back wall, and in its shelves and above it on pegboards and hooks and nails hang his tools: hammers, pliers, wrenches, screwdrivers, files, saw blades, chisels, trowels, hand drills—a vast assortment of particular, specific tools for seemingly every kind of job imaginable. Fishing poles lie horizontal on pegs extending from the walls. A soot-stained potbellied stove is set in one back corner with flashing behind it to reflect the heat. Glass jars full of nails or screws or nuts or bolts hang suspended over the bench, their lids fixed to the bottom of the shelf above. A table saw on wheels sits beside the bench at one end, and at the other Gramps's saddle and saddle blanket rest on a sawhorse, covered by an old canvas tarp. Above the workbench and below the shelf, the long back window of the garage looks out on the meadow and the river, and through it comes the day's light, bent at sharp or dull angles across the garage's interior by the hanging jars.

When I was a boy, I used to spend whole summer mornings and afternoons in the garage, the tall, wooden, barn-style door swung open, admitting a broad curtain of light. I learned each tool's name and purpose and practiced on scrap pieces of wood or metal. In the middle of the afternoon, when the pace down at the store slowed, Gramps and I often went up to the garage, and together we would take on the tasks that he'd set before him: the broken leg of the table in apartment two, a leaky pipe in the bathroom in apartment four, an odd job for someone in town. The list of such tasks was long and never exhausted, which suited us both just fine.

Gramps and I didn't talk much during those times. But the quiet was never awkward or uncomfortable. It was a warm, easy quiet, the kind of quiet that surrounds a person when the country that surrounds them is quiet, when that country is in them deeply and instinctually. We could hear clearly the whirring of the table-saw blade, the spinning of a drill bit, or the clean strike of a hammer driving a nail through wood. We could hear the low rumble of a car or truck out on the highway passing through town slowly. But these sounds were mild interruptions only, not constants, and the quiet would return.

Gramps's way was simply to do the thing once or twice, while I watched, then have me repeat the action. He sometimes made brief corrective statements. "No. Not like that, like this." When I would perform the task well, he would say, "Yes. That's right."

The day begins before dawn. The sky is dark and shadowed with clouds as Oliver takes the bucket to the pump, where he will draw water from the well. He is six. He is small and wiry, his hair blond and uncombed and curly. He is dressed in patched jeans and short sleeves, though it is not yet 5 a.m. He knows what cold is like and this is not cold. At the woodpile beside the low, framed homestead, he can hear his older brother, Syd, thirteen, splitting kindling for the stove. It is the chore Oliver prefers, the chore their father gives to Syd more often than not. But Oliver almost never complains, about anything, and this is not the day for it. He knows that within the hour the first light will color the ridgeline of the mountains to the east and doing so confirm the day. He is ready for it. He has been looking forward to it for weeks.

It is the Fourth of July, 1919, and today the Tremewan family will travel north to Mountain City for the celebration. Oliver's mother is still weak from sickness, the influenza from which she will never recover, but she is going. Oliver's father has led two horses from the barn and hitched them to the wagon. The family will eat breakfast and go. It will be the first time all five children have gone anywhere together. Syd, Edith, Oliver, Ruth, and Lucille. It will take them nearly all day to get to Mountain City from the ranch. As the crow flies, the trip is due north, twenty-five miles, but near halfway a narrow winding canyon with steep volcanic cliffs detours the stage road east. When it reaches Sunflower Flat, it turns back west and follows California Creek to town.

South from the ranch, the road runs fifty miles to Elko, a railroad town, a town which, over the past year, most ranchers dared not go near on account of the influenza epidemic. But Oliver's father and Syd did go, two months earlier. Syd had stumbled and fallen building fence, and the barbed wire had torn a gash below his lip through which he could stick his tongue. Oliver's father drove Syd, feverish in the back of the wagon, all the way up over Adobe Summit and down to Elko, to the hospital, to get him stitched up. Shortly afterwards, Oliver's mother took ill.

Oliver loved watching the road. From it he gathered his knowledge of the outside world. Already that summer, he'd seen hundreds of wild horses trailed past the ranch on their way south. They'd been herded by buckaroos up on the Bruneau desert, and it took the horses all day and into the night to pass by. Before that, Oliver had seen bands of sheep trailed past the ranch north to their summer range and south on their return the next fall. He'd seen them pass by yellowed and smelling like rotten eggs from the sulfur solution in the ditches they were run through, "the dip" they called it, which cured scabies. The

yellowed sheep smell would linger in the air for days after they'd gone. But that was not like those horses. Not like that turmoil of dust that blurred the horizon.

In May, the Williams outfit had lambed at Pie Creek, and passing by on their way north, they left behind seventeen bummer lambs with the Tremewans. Oliver and Ruth bottle-fed them when the rest of their chores were done. Ruth couldn't understand why the lambs had been orphaned, and one afternoon, with one of the lambs stamping its small hooves in her lap and taking the bottle, Ruth asked her brother, "Why don't they pair up, Oliver? Why do they get left behind?"

"Some ewes don't take their young," Oliver said, with authority. "They're like people that way."

Ruth nodded, not understanding, and returned her attention to the lamb that was climbing up and over her to get back to the bottle she held teasingly above her head. Oliver had asked the same question of his father once, and that was the answer he'd been given, and he hadn't forgotten, though he wasn't sure what was meant by it either.

There was a lot Oliver didn't know about, though he couldn't tell his little sister that. For instance, he'd never been to Mountain City. He'd been to few towns in his life, and those few had been only small mining camps with two or three permanent structures, the rest of the town made up of tents and shacks, like Gold Creek or Rowland, down on the Bruneau River.

Syd had been to the Fourth of July in Mountain City and so had Edith. Syd had said there'd be a turkey shoot, and both boys had been practicing: gophers, magpies, coyotes—anything smaller than deer that they hadn't raised or named. Syd had told Oliver that for targets they used to bury actual turkeys up to their necks or put them in a box with only their heads popping out, but for some reason Syd couldn't figure, they'd stopped. They used paper targets now, tagged to haystacks. This news disappointed Oliver. He'd never seen a turkey and wanted to shoot one. He'd seen chuckers and sage hens and shot those, but turkeys were supposed to be even bigger and uglier. And he was bored with tin cans. He wanted whatever it was to *move*.

There would be a dance, and Oliver's mother and the girls had been sewing in the evenings, making dresses for each of them to wear. Edith was eleven, and she could not stop talking about the colors she'd once seen at *the Fourth,* the bright blues and reds and golds that were the colors of a *festival.* Oliver wanted to see those colors, and those fireworks, he wanted to see them. He could hardly imagine from Edith's and Syd's descriptions what they'd be like.

By six they are on the road. Oliver's father has given the reins to Syd, and the young man drives the team north, his father beside him. Oliver sits in the back of the wagon with his mother and his sisters. In subsequent years, Oliver will no longer yearn for the responsibilities his father regularly gives to Syd, or at least not yearn so strongly. By the time Oliver will reach Syd's age, he'll know more work than many men know in their lives, men of privilege and men who by smarts or dumb luck somehow avoid labor. And his father will work him soon enough: haying, breaking horses, building fence, gathering cattle, fixing machinery, irrigating, and in winter sawing blocks of ice from the pond and burying them in the hole behind the homestead to use come summer. But now Oliver's father still considers him a boy, though a boy on the cusp of manhood if only by his sheer desire to enter his father and brother's world.

They pass the Rancho Grande, the PX Ranch. They pass beneath the nine-thousand-foot peaks to the west, which parallel the road north before collapsing suddenly at the mouth of the canyon. They pass cattle and horses in meadows, and newly built ranch houses and cabins, barns and corrals, new for the standard Oliver will come to apply to this country. If a structure is ten, twenty years old, rooted, firm, that to him is new. If a structure has been standing fifty years and is still in use and not just eroding into the landscape, then this qualifies as old and means also that here is a place where people have remained. And in 1919 there are few such structures, for by this standard, near everything is new. And the cabins and ranch houses, barns and corrals, which will suffer weather that takes five years off their lives for every one that mild country might take, these structures have still to prove themselves.

By ten they've made the turn west onto California Creek. The morning is sunny and warm and slips by easily. They see pronghorn antelope, and little Ruth, who is four, spots a great big bird, which Oliver identifies as a golden eagle. They see a few coyotes, which their father, to Oliver's surprise, does not stop to shoot. When Oliver asks why, his father simply replies, "No ranches right around here, and you're never gonna kill them all." They see no deer or elk, which does not surprise Oliver. He knows their summer range to be higher than this low part of the valley.

At the confluence of California Creek and the east fork of the Owyhee, they turn north again, following the river, and in the distance they can see the few buildings that mark the outskirts of Mountain City. The girls chatter louder and more excitedly, to which their mother smiles and says, "Yes, that's it," and, "We'll be there in just a moment." Oliver is as excited as his sisters, but contains it as best he can, though he feels like jumping from the wagon and running the rest of the way to town. His father and brother are quiet, and so he tries his best to be like them.

If these children were from another part of the country, somewhere less isolated, where they would be familiar with the notion of "town" as it was most commonly used, then these children would perhaps have been disappointed by what they next saw. Crumbling foundations. Thin houses and shacks of clapboard, sorry aggregates of wood and tin and tar. Shacks that leaned with the wind and could hardly lean much longer. Only the one wide dirt road, the road on which they traveled, the rest winding rutted and washed out and narrow into the surrounding hills.

But these children are not familiar with any notion of "town" except their own, and Mountain City either meets or surpasses that notion, depending on the child. As the wagon crests the slight rise at the 101 Ranch, beneath which lies the town, shrieks of excitement leap from the throats of Edith and Ruth and Lucille, who is three and is being held up by her older sisters so that she can see. A shriek from Oliver too, who cannot help himself, and even Syd rises slightly from his seat. The road passing now through town is lined with banners. Red. White. Blue. And down the hill near the center of town people mill about, hundreds of them. Oliver's mother is smiling, broadly, fully, and Oliver sees her and knows her at that moment precisely to be happy and this recognition will never leave him. The hollows beneath pronounced cheekbones, the eyes darkened and ringed and sunken, the neck leading thinned to a body thinned by the pneumonia that followed without respite the influenza. All transformed by the wonder that inhabits her children so strongly it suffuses and overwhelms her and will last the day.

Mountain City is not a town or city or anything else. Mountain City is copper and a little silver and less gold. Mountain City is a state of flux and impermanence.

In 1870, in only its second year of infancy, Mountain City swells from log dugouts in a meadow beside a river to a place of hundreds and later thousands. That year W. J. Hill of the *Owyhee Avalanche,* a Silver City, Idaho, newspaper, describes the town of 130 buildings, one half of which are canvas tents, as having twenty saloons, nine stores, two rooming houses, two bakeries, two breweries, four blacksmith shops, two livery stables, two drugstores, one stationery store, one fruit store, one paint shop, an assay office, a real estate office, a bank, a stage office, a post office, one first-class hotel, and one "love store," or "hurdy-gurdy house."

In 1882 it becomes a place of twenty. Sixteen whites and four Chinese. A place suddenly vacant, as if a victim of natural disaster and not economics, a place lost, baffled by fortune, by lack of fortune, by fortune untapped or too difficult to tap or too hidden. In 1904, hundreds come again, not thousands this time, but hundreds, and hundreds no less cautious or wary, who had not learned the lessons of the place and its short history, or learned but forgotten, or learned but chose to ignore the learning. In 1919, it is a place again of ten or twenty. And so Mountain City is a place of repetition, a Western archetype for hope and failed hope and failure. Its sisters and brothers live on the other side of the Bull Run Mountains, the Jarbridge Mountains. They live a few or many miles up the road or down. And Mountain City is a place in waiting because it knows itself. It knows its bloodstream is lined still with metals for which people will come again.

And on the morning of the fifth of July, 1919, all the tents in the meadow along the river will be taken down and taken home, and the town and the ten or twenty will again be left to themselves, waiting.

The sun has passed its apex in the sky, and instruments play in the distance, a snare drum, a trumpet or bugle. Syd has parked the wagon in the meadow, and he and Oliver and their father stake out the tent while Edith and her mother lay out a blanket. Ruth and Lucille roll and play in the grass near the bank of the river, which meanders through the meadow.

The family joins the crowd of people at the town's center. Booths line the street and from each come calls and shouts and enticements. The booths sell hamburgers and sausages and ice cream and there are games of all kinds: sack races and arm-wrestling contests; soda bottles arranged in a circle and rings to toss; balloons on a board and darts to throw; a horseshoe pitch around which many people have formed an oval gallery. At one booth an old Shoshone woman and several small children. Oliver thinks the children must be her grandchildren or great-grandchildren for they are his age and younger and she is the oldest woman he's ever seen. The Indians sell moccasins and cradle boards and beaded jewelry. Around the periphery of the booth a few boys and girls are staring at the old woman, and Oliver can't tell whether they stare at her age or her nature. Oliver is used to Indians. A Shoshone man named Joe has been helping them put up hay at their ranch. He is quiet and he is good help.

For a time the family moves from booth to booth, all of them together, watching and trying the different games. Ruth and Lucille hold their father's hands, and Oliver holds his mother's hand, which he does not usually do because Syd never does, but she has reached for his hand and he has taken it in his.

They walk a short ways down the road to watch the saddle bronc riding. Onlookers have gathered along the fence of a corral and the Tremewans join them. Oliver wants to know why his father isn't entering the competition.

"Dad, you broke every horse we got and plenty we don't. Why aren't you in there?"

"Oliver, I've been bucked off and kicked enough in my life to know better than to start doing it for fun. Fifteen years ago, maybe, but not now. And these fellas aren't breaking horses."

Here his father pauses, as if thinking on whether or not to continue. He is not given to speaking more than a few sentences at once. But he sees the eagerness in his boy. The boy loves horses. His father continues, "These horses won't get broke. You got to halter-train them and lead them and let them get used to that. Then you saddle them up and let them loose in the corral to try and buck it off. Then you saddle them up again, cinch it down tight, and let them buck and kick again. You know that, right?"

Oliver nods. He knows that.

"Son, they got to get good and tired out. *Then* you ride them. These fellas aren't doing none of that. They're just jumping on. Half these boys'll have broke ribs by the end of the afternoon. That's all they'll be breaking."

Oliver finds his father to be right, for the most part. Most of the men attempting to ride the broncs are young, in their late teenage years, and most of them seem determined either to demonstrate or to elaborate upon Oliver's father's prediction. The young cowboys are bucked off just as they leave the chute, or kicked, or stepped on, or catch their hands in their saddle ropes and have their bodies dragged around the corral hanging from the stuck arms like rag dolls. But one particular young man, a cowboy from down on the Bruneau named Riley Chambers, never once gets bucked off. He rides each horse under control, while they buck and jump and do all they can, and after ten seconds or so, he just lets go, jumps off, lands on his feet or close to it, and makes for the fence. Oliver is amazed and he wants someday to be as good with horses as Riley Chambers. He leaves the corral in a state of pure excitement.

At five the turkey shoot starts. Roughly thirty people enter, Oliver and Syd and their father among them. The targets, coal outlines on paper of some strange animal half-resembling a bird, are pinned to several haystacks at a distance of one hundred yards. A circle is inscribed inside the outlined figure, and the closer one's bullet to the circle, the better the shot. By the end of the first round, after which the ten best shots are to back up a distance of another twenty-five yards, the contest is over, and everyone knows it, participants and onlookers. Syd's five bullets have all but one entered the circle, and the stray has not strayed far. Oliver and his father shoot well, and Oliver is by several years the youngest of all the entrants. But Syd takes the day, and he takes it the only way he knows how. Quietly. He doesn't say anything, but gives to his mother a sort of half grin. Plenty of people talk for him. About his age. About his eye, how good it is, talking about it as if there's only one of them and not a pair, as if an *eye* is something most people lack, "That boy's got an *eye* on him," as if it's something strange or fantastic or alien, "Did you see the *eye* on that boy?" Oliver is proud of his brother but unsurprised. Every day of his life, he's felt the heat of Syd's confidence radiating beside him. Syd's parents are proud of both their sons and they tell them so and each son says thank you. And not long after, the wonder of the event dissolves into the day as the rest of the wonders have done, and it is dusk.

A dance in the evening. For the occasion a platform built by a few of the ten or twenty of Mountain City. On poles surrounding the platform, carbide lanterns. Light for a town of metal. Light used underground. Light needing less oxygen than candles so that the men keep canaries with them beneath the earth. So that when the canaries die they know to get the hell out. And this carbide light blurs the edges of the canopy of stars above the dance.

A woman plays a fiddle and leans on one leg and taps the foot of the other. And her husband or brother or someone she loves and who loves her keeps time also but with his hands on the upturned bottom of a wash bucket. Oliver does not know the tunes except for a few that his mother sometimes sings in the evenings at bedtime. But his parents know many, and he sees them smile at each other in the first few bars of a new song, and he realizes then that they have danced together before. Still, it surprises him to see his father, with a smirk on his face that Oliver will never see again, approach his mother and ask her in a comic voice Oliver does not know, "Rose, may I please have this dance?" And she responds, "Yes, Charlie, you may." And the two of them dance, Oliver's mother so light that she seems without substance or mass. And Syd and Oliver dance with their sisters, Edith and little Ruth and littler Lucille, each girl having earlier changed into her homemade dress as their mother has done. And some people looking on see this couple and their children and think those children beautiful. Beautiful not because they are so clean or well-groomed or because their features arc more than ordinary, for they are not. But beautiful because these people see the children's mother in her sickness and see her clearly, their seeing directed by neither hope nor its wanting, and these people sense that this family's time together is short, and that here is their time now, and that it belongs to them as does the most private heirloom belong to one family and never another. And in this recognition the children become beautiful, as all such children must become. And in Oliver's father too there is a sense of time and its brevity and his family's brief ownership of that time. And in Oliver's mother these senses are deepest. But still, now, despite this, she is happy and they dance and Oliver will not forget.

On the morning of July 12, 1919, Rose Tremewan died of pneumonia, suffocating quietly in her sleep. The sky outside was a bright, light blue. No clouds, nothing to shade the Tremewans from the clarity of what they had to face. Oliver did not speak that day. His father came out of the house and over to where Oliver was sitting alone in the yard. He knelt down and put a hand on his son's small shoulder and then Oliver knew, and he nodded and looked away.

Hours later, when Oliver returned home from wandering the foothills alone, it was evening. Syd was waiting for him. Their father had taken their mother into Elko, and their sisters had gone to a neighbor's house down the road. The boys would go there now.

He would not say anything, but it seemed to Oliver that deep in his gut a coiled spring had slipped its bracings, and his insides were flying apart.

Behind Tremewan's Store, a dirt road leads into a draw, and on either side of the draw, before the hills begin upward to their crests, small, low houses, in varying stages of neglect and abandonment, stand boarded up and empty. Inside these houses, pictures hang neatly on walls above grass growing through floorboards. On bureaus and bedside tables, plastic faces of small General Electric alarm clocks fix the past to each individual desertion. Outside, sage has reclaimed fenced-in yards, and cans and bottles and weathered cardboard lie strewn about like island debris. Shingles lie upturned in the dirt like resigned turtles. A wrought-iron headboard leans against a porch. A white Westinghouse icebox, its mouth open, breathes into weeds. With sagging, sloping roofs, these houses droop and shrug, their colors grayed by wind and weather. They outnumber the inhabited houses and trailer homes down along the highway four or five to one.

No one visits these houses, except the field mice, whose visits are practical and self-serving. Beneath couches and chairs the mice store string and plastic wrappers and small metal things. From the comfort of living rooms they enjoy rainstorms and blizzards and leave their droppings where they please. In some rooms, the droppings have accumulated greatly, so that the worn wood floor or rug is altogether obscured, and the powerful, ironic smell of abandonment and burrow hangs in the fetid air like fog. At night, hawks fly through broken windows, sailing room to room among the bare cupboards and peeling wallpaper, and the mice, trembling, huddle beneath their couches and chairs.

No one thinks of these houses much, except for the few people who remember when the houses were not like this. Like the widows. Bobbie and Margaret and Dorothy, in their trailer homes beside the highway. And Rosella, in her trailer home on the hill above the draw, looking down on the past.

When the widows think of these houses, they do so in a way that you might not guess. They don't want them cleaned up or repaired or lived in. They like them the way they are. When they think of these houses, they think: Here is what has remained. These houses and us.

Basque surnames often refer to where people live, to places, to houses, and to the relationships between places or houses. For example, Goikoextea means "the house above." Goiko = "above," and exte = "house" or "home." Iturriaga means "the place by the fountain." Iturri = "fountain," and aga = "place."

Arriaga	Place covered with stones
Arteaga	Place of oaks
Bengoechea	House farther below

Echegaray	Upper house
Erquiaga	Place of linden trees
Extemendi	Mountain which belongs to the house
Goyeneche	Highest house
Lasaga	Place by the stream
Madariaga	Place of pear trees
Pagoaga	Place of beech trees
Sistiaga	Place of bulrushes
Urrengoechea	Following house
Zuluaga	Place of holes

It's not hard to imagine what these names suggest about heritage and rootedness and belonging, about history, about the *homeplace,* a place where multiple generations live under the same roof, take meals together at the same table their ancestors sat down to, ancestors whose pictures grace the mantle, who died on beds still slept in each night. For it must be a distinct imagination, a unique cultural mind, that names itself "Place covered with stones" or "Place of holes." It is an imagination which serves the land and the things on the land more than the individual. A people with names like "Following house" or "House farther below" can't even refer to themselves except in the context of others, and other places, except in the context of community.

All the names in this list are taken from a cultural anthropologist's book about Basque immigrants in America, and so these names are thousands of miles away from home, away from themselves. The Goicoechea family I know lives on a ranch off the Mountain City highway. The Goicocccheas are good ranchers, good stewards of the land they've owned and managed for more than seventy years. But their house isn't above or below or beside any other houses. It is along a stream, but they're not about to change their name to Lasaga. Their name has not, in its literal sense, lost its meaning. It still means what it means. But what's lost is its metaphoric bond, its figurative connection to landscape. Cultural identity, the homeplace, and the relationship between cultural identity and homeplace are lost. Three generations from that homeplace, I've lived in twenty-one places in twelve states in twenty-seven years.

In the boom and bust mining towns of Nevada and the West, where drastic population swings, like the weather, are predictably unpredictable, the trailer home is a symbol of a certain kind of progress. People have learned something. They've realized that the resources their jobs and lives depend on will someday run out, and they're saying to themselves: Chances are, this won't last forever. A few years if we're lucky. Let's get a house that moves so that when the price of gold (or silver or copper or whatever) goes to shit, we can get the hell out.

More than half of the thirty-three people in Mountain City live in trailer homes. On both sides of the highway, the trailer homes sit beside and between old houses used now for storage. These trailer homes are paneled with yellow or green aluminum, and a few of the newer models have a stained wood veneer. Large picture windows look out on gardens and fenced yards and trees, and sliding doors open onto small decks covered by awnings.

Unlike most places in Nevada, where nomadism rules and trailer homes abound, these trailer homes arrived after the bust. The people in trailer homes in Mountain City aren't living in a state of waiting, prepared for the worst, their maps in drawers ready to spread out on the kitchen table. The mobile homes in Mountain City are permanent.

The reasons behind the irony are simple and economic. None of the old, empty houses in Mountain City is fit to live in. The wind doesn't just whistle through them, it dances and sings. Few are better than barns. And no one in Mountain City can afford to have a new house built. Even if they could afford to haul all the building materials the eighty-four miles from Elko, they couldn't pay for both the labor and the daily round-trip transportation costs of the construction crew.

For the widows, Rosella and Bobbie and Dorothy and Margaret, trailer homes are more practical than new houses. Trailer homes are smaller, with less space to feel absences. And trailer homes are far more practical than their old houses next door. Trailer homes are double-walled and insulated and without drafts to find and mend in fall, before the chill comes.

In its 130-year history, Mountain City has supported several houses of prostitution. The last one closed sometime in the late 1940s, after the Rio Tinto busted. The building is still standing. Each of its six upstairs rooms has two doors, one opening in from the hallway, and another opening onto an outside staircase in the back. In the sixties, the building was moved over the mountains to the Petan Ranch. It's a bunkhouse now, its history permeating ranch hands' dreams.

Like those of many Nevadans, Mel's position on the subject of "girls stores" isn't a moral one. It's entirely economical, influenced by his years as a grocery man.

"The great thing about it is there's no inventory. You have something. You sell it. And then you still have it. That's good business."

A wealthy, middle-aged California couple comes into the store. The man's wearing a suit, which, in Mountain City, is like wearing a Halloween costume. The woman is wearing more glittery ornaments than a Christmas tree. Her eyelids are mauve. She glances around, notes the rustic, provincial charm.

"I really like your little store."

"How much do you like it?" Mel asks sharply. His eyes narrow.

"Quite a lot."

"No, I mean, how *much*? There's a price for everything, you know. And me and the wife, well, we've been thinking about unloading this pork and beans operation, moving to the big city, soak up some of that culture you got there."

"No. Not really, would you?"

"Really. Would *you* be interested in this place? Free groceries. T-bone steaks every night." Mel is insistent, pushy.

"Well, no," she says, her enthusiasm gone. She doesn't understand Mel's tone.

"Oh. Oh. Okay. Just thought I'd ask." Mel nods knowingly to himself, like he's just proven a point.

The couple buys two bottled waters and then they leave.

"Did you see me give her the old 'aw shucks' routine?" Mel asks me.

"I saw it."

"You don't like that too much, do you? You think it's mean."

"I didn't say that."

I've seen Mel do this before. He doesn't do it too often, because he knows it drives away customers, but at times he can't seem to help himself.

Over the past few years, for some reason, I've taken to playing the role of Mel's conscience. We have these conversations frequently, where Mel asks me, "You don't think I should say that, do you?" Most of the time, I'm righteous in my responses, indignant, as if my uncle needs "civilizing," and I'm the one for the job. Sometimes, after Mel says something insensitive, he looks my way slyly, and winks. He's trying to get a rise out of me, to see if I'll jump on my soapbox.

But in this particular case, I didn't like the couple any more than Mel did. I had already imagined them back at their gated community, saying, "You should have seen the quaint country store we discovered in Nevada," as if the store, and our ingenuous, uncomplicated lives in it, existed solely for their aesthetic pleasure, for their sentimental appropriation.

"Did you see folks like them all the time back east?" Mel asks.

"Snobs, you mean?"

"Snobs is a good word."

"Sure. Plenty like that. Plenty my age, too."

"That fella in the suit sure was something."

"A real stoic," I say.

"Yeah, and besides that, he didn't say a word." Mel smiles. This is another game Mel plays, another version of his "aw shucks" routine. If I say that the wild horses down on the Bruneau desert aren't indigenous to the area, Mel will say, "Yeah, and besides that, they're not from around here, either."

Last winter, an Iranian man stayed for a few weeks in one of my grandparents' apartments. He was a small man, utterly reserved, with coal hair and skin a shade or two darker than Mel's. He was an engineer, working on a project up at the hospital in Owyhee. One of the only things he told us about himself was that he would become a U.S. citizen in a few months.

It was late November, and the temperature in Mountain City most nights had dropped below zero. One morning, Char, that was his name, walked down to the store because his car wouldn't start. He needed to get to work.

"Do you have a block heater?" Mel asked him, after listening to Char explain the situation in broken English.

Char didn't understand.

"A block heater is something you install in your car to warm the antifreeze, to keep it circulating, so your engine doesn't get too cold. So it will start when the temperature's low."

Char nodded and said, "You have a block heater." He meant in the store.

"We sure do, over in automotive." Mel led Char to the shelf, handed him the box.

"You install it," Char said, and handed the box back to Mel.

Maybe Char intended this as a question, as a favor, and not as a demand, but it didn't come out that way. There was nothing ingratiating about it. It was an imperative. Perhaps there was a cultural misunderstanding. Or perhaps, for Char, Mel, in his green apron, belonged to a different social class than an engineer, and Char simply expected this kind of service from Mel. Maybe that's a crude hypothesis. Either way, Mel installed the block heater that morning, out in the bitter cold, wearing a winter coat over his green apron. He removed the lower radiator hose of Char's old Buick. With his pocketknife he cut out a three-inch band from its middle, clamped the block heater in its place, and reattached the hose to the radiator and the engine. The block heater's plug required an extension cord long enough to run upstairs to an outlet in Char's apartment, and Mel loaned Char one from Gramps's garage. Char drove to work before ten.

It wouldn't be accurate to say this service was free. Char paid a price for it, though I don't think he ever knew it. Maybe he did. Afterwards, Mel referred to Char as the Shah or the Shah of Iran. *There goes the Shah on his magic carpet. They don't come equipped with block heaters in the desert.* For variation, he substituted *camel* for *magic carpet. Them camels have built-in radiators but no block heaters. No need.* I offered token resistance for a day or two, played the role of Mel's conscience. *You shouldn't say that.* After that, I laughed, played along.

————

Melvin Basañez has a gift for languages. He speaks five: Basque, English, Spanish, Shoshone, and Paiute.

Mel grew up speaking Basque at home and English at school, and he learned Spanish from the Mexicans who worked on the railroad with his father. After Mel and Lou came to Mountain City in 1961 to work for my grandparents, Mel learned Shoshone and Paiute. He learned greetings and good-byes and used them when his Indian customers came in and out the door.

"Ha ga nee nak?" he'd say, which is Shoshone, and means, "How you doing?"

"Pata cha oy," Wayne Dick would answer, and this means, "Hungover."

Or he'd ask, *"How man e wan?"* This is Paiute and means, "How are you?"

And Myra Harney would answer, *"Pee sha so na mee,"* meaning, "Feeling good."

When Mel heard an expression he didn't know, he'd say, "Now, how does that go?"

He claims he is fluent in neither Shoshone nor Paiute, but I have seen him carry on conversations of more than an hour. On the reservation, they call Mel the Pyrenees Paiute. Mel has been in the airport in Reno, at a basketball game in Salt Lake City, and at a restaurant in Boise, when he's heard someone shout after him, "Hey, Pyrenees Paiute!" He rarely catches it the first time because he's outside the world of the store. But the second time he catches on. It's one of his Indian customers from the reservation, calling after him, coming over to talk to him, say hello.

Mel didn't learn the Indians' languages so he could get their business. He had their business. There's nowhere else to go for a hundred miles. He learned their languages because he loves to talk. He loves sounds. He learned their languages to get to know them.

Sam Harney and Joe Blackhat are standing around the front counter talking Shoshone with Mel. Both Indians are old cowboys, and they stand bowlegged and awkward, and, leaning forward, each rests one or both hands on the counter. They're talking with Mel about horses or cows or something to do with horses or cows, when a pretty white woman comes through the front door. It's clear to each of them immediately that the woman is not from the area. She's tall and blond and long-legged and maybe thirty, exactly the kind of woman they rarely see. As she makes her way through the store, Mel and Sam and Joe go back to talking, but sluggishly. After a few minutes, the woman comes back looking confused.

"What are you hunting, ma'am?" Mel asks.

"Huh?"

"Can I help you find something?"

"Where do you keep your Tylenol? I've got a bit of a headache."

"That wall over there beneath the whiskey." Mel points over by the north wall, and the woman nods her head. "We keep all the head-related remedies right by the liquor for our customers' convenience." Mel winks at the two Indians.

"A wise policy," the woman jokes back.

"We think so. We got quite a pastime going."

"But it seems like there's so much else to do."

"It's a regular carnival. Hard to figure why anybody'd take to the bottle." Mel rings up the Tylenol. "Where you headed?"

"I'm visiting some relatives in Boise."

"Coming from where?"

"Las Vegas."

"Lost Wages," Mel says. "I go down there every couple three years and help those casinos pay for all them lights."

"Quite a few people do that. You're not alone."

"That's good to know."

"Thanks again." The woman turns for the door.

"Hope that Tylenol does the trick." As the door swings shut behind her, Mel says in a lowered voice to Sam and Joe, *"San be nabon!"*

The two old Indians start laughing. Sam puts a hand back on the counter to steady himself. Joe's laughter turns to a cough; his eyes water.

"You fellas better get headed back down the road," Mel says. "I don't allow heart attacks in here."

"Okay, we're going," says Sam. Joe's still coughing. "See you later, Basco."

The two men leave.

"What'd you say?" I ask.

"San be nabon!" Mel says again, this time with more emphasis. "Now you got to be careful when you say this. Be selective with your audience. *San be nabon* in Shoshone means, essentially, 'She looks good as she walks away,' which a guy could translate a little different if he wanted to, but there's really no need. The Shoshone sums it up nicely, I think, and not all that rude either. Those old Indians love that expression. And they love me saying

it. That blonde swivels around to go and they're thinking it, and then here's this Basco saying it. They love that."

Thirteen miles of narrow, winding canyon road separate Mountain City and Owyhee. About a thousand people live in and around Owyhee, and it has a hospital and a school, but there's no grocery store. Over the past fifty years, there have been several different stores there, but all have failed for various reasons—mismanagement, theft, arson. For all their shopping, the residents of Owyhee must make the twenty-six-mile round-trip drive through the canyon to Mountain City.

There are only fifty or sixty people in the Mountain City area who don't live on the reservation. That's not enough people to support the store, or to support it as it is now, anyway. Without the reservation, the store would go under.

At the beginning of each month, more than half of the citizens of Duck Valley come to Tremewan's Store to cash payroll checks and Indian General Assistance checks. The closest bank is in Elko, eighty-four miles south of Mountain City. The store cashes thousands and thousands of dollars of checks. Most people pay off their credit for the previous month and charge more groceries.

Most people don't grocery-shop where they bank, and if they do, the bank teller isn't running the checkout register. That way, no one person knows how much money a person receives each month, where that money comes from, and how that money is spent.

An Indian woman with a baby in her arms comes in the store at 9 a.m. She is young, about twenty, and she looks tired. She does not take a basket or a cart. She carries each item in her one free hand and sets it on the front counter. One by one, they accumulate: milk, cereal, cheese, peanut butter, eggs, bread. She pays for all of these with a WIC check. Women, Infants, and Children. The check indicates exactly the kind and amount of the items she may buy, down to the ounces of cereal, the pounds of cheese. When that transaction is done, two more things: a bag of Doritos, and a "suitcase" of Budweiser—a twenty-four-can pack. She signs the back of her Indian General Assistance check, I cash it for her, and she hands back one of the twenties. I help carry her groceries and the suitcase out to the car. An Indian man with a red bandanna wrapped around his head waits behind the wheel. The engine is running, coughing white clouds of exhaust into the cold morning air.

When Gramps bought the store from an old Basco named Manuel Bastida in 1958, it had been only a few years since the repeal of a federal law prohibiting the sale of alcohol to Indians. Before the repeal, Bastida had sold alcohol to the Indians anyway, stuffing the bottles in sacks of coal used for stove fuel.

One of the first things Gramps did after he bought the store was apply for a liquor license. Within weeks, the license came, and business steadily improved. I once asked Gramps about this, about the fact that for years he'd profited by selling alcohol to Indians, who, as everybody knew, had a higher percentage of alcoholism than did whites or most other groups. Wasn't he contributing to this? Wasn't the store part of the problem?

Gramps answered my question with a few questions of his own. "Should I have just sold alcohol to whites? Should I have just sold alcohol to the whites and Indians I figured could handle their liquor? Should I have not sold liquor at all, to anybody?"

The Duck Valley Senior Citizens are making their weekly trip to Tremewan's Store. Thursday. One p.m. About thirty senior citizens arrive in a fancy new transit bus equipped with a wheelchair lift. Though many of the seniors use walkers or canes, not one uses a wheelchair. But most all of them ride the lift.

Dressed in shawls and sturdy dresses of cotton or polyester, most of the women are tiny, frail, bent figures, their faces creased with deep wrinkles. There are only a few men. I once asked Lou how old she thought Mamie Thomas was, and she said, "She was a little old lady when Mel and I came thirty-five years ago, so she's probably anywhere from a hundred to a hundred fifty."

The senior citizens' visit is one of Mel's favorite times of the week. He speaks with each of them, in either Paiute or Shoshone, and they smile and laugh at the way he says certain things, and for nearly an hour the sounds of two of the hemisphere's oldest languages carry over and through and down the aisles of Tremewan's Store. It is a wonder to hear. And beneath the language and its words shuffle slow steps, like fine-grained sandpaper over smooth wood.

It is one of my favorite times as well, and as the bus pulls up, I look forward to seeing them all, but some I look forward to seeing especially: Mamie, who is the oldest person I have ever seen, and not quiet either, like you might expect from someone so old. She's sharp, with a lively sense of humor. She calls the senior citizens the War Party, and when she comes in the door, she narrows her eyes and looks devilishly at Mel, who has one hand pressed down on his head, protecting his fine Basco hair. George Harney, one of the tribe's oldest men, his hand always supporting his wife Ethel's elbow though it is he who seems closer to falling down. Redora Atkins, who has already been to the store that morning with her daughter. Redora comes often. She will return that evening with another daughter or grand-daughter and great-grandchildren. Of all the people of the Duck Valley Reservation, I feel I know Redora best, though all we exchange are hellos and smiles and a few joking comments here and there. I know none of the Indians who come to the store in the way that Mel and Lou and my grandparents know so many. I am familiar with them and know most of their names. I am kind and so are they, but more than this way of knowing takes time, and I've been here only off and on my whole life.

Voyne stands rigid on the front porch of the store. It's December and the early-morning temperature hasn't yet climbed to zero. He wears an old plaid work jacket, worn jeans and boots, and a bright yellow ski cap and Gore-Tex gloves that Mel has given him. He looks mismatched, out of place, like a bum about to board a lift at a fancy resort. Because he hardly moves, he can't be warm. I don't think he feels the cold anymore, or if he does, I don't think he cares. He stands just outside the border of the window, so that from inside the store we can't see him. I don't know who he does this for, himself or us, but it doesn't matter. We know he's there. He'll stand there all day. Sometimes he leans against the brick wall. Voyne is a Paiute Indian from the Duck

Valley Reservation. They say he's in his fifties, but he looks as old as Gramps, his face weathered and corrugated and lifeless.

When Mel, my cousin Mitch, and I arrive this morning to open the store, Voyne is waiting. Someone, probably on the way south to Elko, has given him a ride from Owyhee. I have never seen Voyne drive. A few minutes after we turn on the lights and unlock the front door, Voyne comes in. Mel waits at the front counter.

"Pick this up, Mel?" Voyne asks in the slurred, nearly incoherent speech that is always his.

"Can't do that, Voyne. I told you yesterday, no more credit until you pay off your bill."

Mel doesn't talk Paiute with Voyne.

Voyne rocks back on his heels, as if registering a blow. He asks Mel a second and third time, pausing only briefly after each attempt, and with each rejection he appears dumbfounded. The bottle of wine Voyne's body needs sits on the top shelf of the store's north wall. Voyne looks over to the bottle between rejections. It is dark green with an orange label. Gibson Port. It costs $3.59, the cheapest wine we sell.

In lighter times, maybe after a jail release when Voyne is more dried out, Mel sometimes jokes with him about his uncompromising devotion to wine. Voyne won't drink beer or liquor. In this one respect, he is single-mindedly dedicated.

"You have nearly three dollars here, Voyne. You can get two beers for that, you know."

Voyne shakes his head and slides the change back into his cupped hand.

"You're a purist, you know that, Voyne. A true wino. The last of a dying breed."

Voyne returns to the porch to beg, the humor lost on him, as always, and so it is always cruel, like teasing a stupid child.

Each month, after we cut Voyne off from credit, he begs on the front porch, and he begs until he gets the $3.59, though he doesn't know when that is. His mind is so addled from years of alcoholism that he can't count change. He spreads the coins out on the counter, and we add them for him. I think Voyne is too far gone to feel the shame in this. I hope so. I hope the stupor insulates him from self-awareness. I can't bear to think what he otherwise might feel.

When I was a boy, there were more winos at Tremewan's Store, all Indians from the reservation. The store had benches on the front porch then, and they would sit drinking all day, their bottles wrapped in brown paper sacks. Something about the way they sat there frightened me, something about their laughter, which greeted me as I came up the porch steps. Something was funny, but I didn't know what. I had to summon all my nerve just to walk past them through the front door.

At some point, Mel and Lou removed the benches and prohibited drinking on the porch. Since then, one of the monthly chores has been to sweep up the shards of glass from the bottles broken against the back wall behind the store by the old incinerator, the winos' chosen place of exile. Voyne is one of the few left to keep up squatters' rights.

I can tell the time of month by the look in Voyne's eyes. On the first of each month, they're fixed with fevered anticipation. Payday. Mel says: "Uncle Sam's throwing a big party for Voyne today." Voyne receives a check from Indian General Assistance, and he comes to the store to cash it. He pays off his credit, which is always around a hundred dollars because that's when we cut him off. He buys a bottle of wine, takes it out back, drinks it, comes back and buys another.

A week into his bender, Voyne's eyes turn mean, crazy, and he is dangerous. A few years ago, he stabbed a man in the phone booth outside the store. He didn't know the man, a geologist for the Forest Service, and he didn't want to use the phone. Another time, when Colon Perry, Mountain City's deputy sheriff, attempted to arrest Voyne for urinating on the highway in the middle of town, Voyne attacked him, punching him in the face and wrestling him to the ground. At these times, the stench of alcohol hangs over Voyne like a storm cloud threatening. Every pore of his body is saturated with drink. Early in such a day, we may let him in, sell what we know will twist him into something hardly human, and hope he returns right then to Owyhee. Sometimes, we'll sell to him only if his ride is waiting. Later in the day, if we're watching the door, we won't let him in. The wagons are circled. We are wary and tense and anxiously aware of the power he has over us, the power we, in many ways, have given him.

When Voyne's eyes have grown opaque, it is the middle of the month, and he is broke and benign. We now let Voyne charge a bottle of wine a day. He might charge a few groceries also and will usually go back home with whoever brought him. Near the end of the month, Voyne's eyes have gone slack, and the emptiness that inhabits them is profound, like dry, unbroken plains seen from the foothills of mountains, the barren world he knows he must not enter. He is not sober yet, but he is desperate and he begs.

We know Voyne far more than most people know the beggars they see on city streets and in subway stations on their way to and from work. We know how much money he receives each month and from where. We know when it's gone and why. We know who looks after him and where he lives. We regulate Voyne's drinking. We cut him off, not for his own well-being, but to ensure that he can pay his debt, so that we will not lose money. We have never spoken a real word to him in our lives. He has nothing to say. He is, to us, the embodiment of a stereotype, a caricature, a distortion. He is not himself. To us, he is not, and never has been, an uncle, or great-uncle, to a young boy or girl. He is not an elder's son or nephew or grandson. He is a figment of our imagination, a ghost. We don't know him at all.

At five o'clock each day Mel pours his first highball into a tall, clear glass. Ice, Black Velvet, 7UP from a small seven-ounce can. He drinks behind the butcher's counter. He sets the glass on the polished top of the stainless-steel meat grinder, and he slices ham, baloney, cheese. He packages hot dogs or hamburger. He sips whiskey. A sign Mel has hung on the wall behind him reads, NO WORKIN' DURING DRINKIN' HOURS. It's a rule he can't follow. He'll pour a second drink before we close at six.

If Kenny Kohones or Larry Otheim or any one of a few other men happen to be in the store in the hour before closing, Mel will pour them a highball, without offering, and set it out for them on the meat counter. The two men will drink and chat, and Larry or Kenny or whoever will stand a little to the side so Mel can take orders. One such time, as Lou walked past the men on her way to the front, she muttered, "We ought to get barstools."

Mel called after her, "I want the kind that spin around."

Mel doesn't offer drinks to Indians. Once, when he mismarked Jim Rides Horse's pork chops, writing down the weight and not the price, he held up his highball and said, *"Son hebe,"* which is Shoshone and means, "Too much to drink."

"I'm on my way," Jim said.

"Don't forget to pack your suitcase."

"No need. These ones come packed and ready to go."

"They make it easy."

"Yeah. More convenient."

"Just don't do all your unpacking on the drive home."

Another time, Mel asked Jim Rides Horse if he was still bartending at night for Eddie at the Miner's Club.

"As far as I know," Jim said.

"I'm gonna have to talk with Eddie about that," Mel said. "He should know better than to leave Indians in charge of the fort."

"Someone might get scalped," Jim said.

"That's what I'm getting at," Mel said. "You know, I do some bartending of my own back here at the meat counter."

"Looks like you pour pretty stiff."

"Pretty stiff."

"There goes all your profits."

"You ain't just a-kidding."

I sometimes call Mel Five o'Clock Charlie, after the crazy North Korean pilot on the television show M*A*S*H who always dropped his bombs on the dump or on someone's unoccupied jeep. Charlie always seemed about to crash, in kamikaze fashion, into the camp, before finally puttering off into the distance. Charlie never hurt anyone. I don't mean to take the analogy this far. I'm just trying to break the tension that ends the day. Lou and Mitch don't say much to Mel between five and six.

Mel will pour a third drink and horse it down quickly before we all leave the store around six-fifteen. After closing, Lou and Mitch each drive up separately to Grandma and Gramps's place for dinner. Mel and I walk. Some nights each of Mel's steps follows a different line.

When Mel was sixteen and starting to court Lou, she invited him over to dinner with the whole Tremewan family. He'd just moved that year to Elko from Winnemucca, where he'd known everybody in town, where people were used to his talkative personality. The Tremewan dinner table was a bit quieter than the long dining table at the Martin Hotel, where some old sheepherder was always telling a joke. Mel sensed immediately after sitting down, after studying Gramps (he wasn't Gramps yet) for a moment, that the Tremewans were a tough crowd and that a Basco joke might not go over too well. He tried to contain himself. He was nervous. Under the table, his hands flopped in his lap like fish on the bottom of a boat. He couldn't help himself. He kept asking for things.

Would you pass the salt, please?

I'd take some more of that salad.

How about the pepper now?

I'm like a runt with litter syndrome. Another pork chop?

Them potatoes are real good, could you send them my way?

Boy, I'm drinking like a sailor. Hope I can walk outa here. I better have another glass of that iced tea.

He went on and on. Grandma (she wasn't Grandma yet) and the four Tremewan sisters just looked at one another, smiled, and waited for the inevitable. After about a half hour, Gramps set down his fork and knife, glared at Mel, and said: *Would you shut up and eat!*

Mel told me once that if he could have known, at that moment, at sixteen years old, that he would eat almost every supper for the rest of his life with Gramps, he probably would have found the nearest mine shaft and jumped in. He said trying to get Gramps to warm up to him was a lot like the stare-down contests little kids have. The one who blinked first lost. In this case, Mel was trying to get Gramps to smile. Mel said it took a long time, but he finally got him.

This Basco kid I know from Winnemucca went off to college this year, and he came back the other day for the holidays. Said he'd learned all sorts of new things. So I said, Okay, like what? And he said, Well, for one, I know a lot more geography than I did before. And I said, That sounds good, like for example? And he said, For example, I've learned the capitals of all the states. Go ahead, ask me, he said. And I said, Okay, what's the capital of Wyoming? He said that was one of the easier ones. W.

Mel's mom now waitressed every night at the Star Hotel, and since his dad wasn't around much at dinnertime, Grandma insisted that Mel eat at the Tremewans'. In fact, if he failed to show, Grandma would call Mel's mom and ask if anything was the matter. Were Mel and Lou having trouble? Was something wrong? Mel said he ate every single dinner his senior year over at the Tremewans', even Thanksgiving and Christmas.

The winter that Gramps turned eighty-four it took him three full months to recover from his pneumonia. Every morning he stayed behind at the house while I walked down to the store alone. His doctor wouldn't allow him even the briefest exposure to freezing temperatures. He couldn't walk down to the store, shovel the walk, or work in the garage. He sat most of the day covered with a quilt in his chair in the living room, his cough scraping the quiet like a plow blade on frozen asphalt. I wasn't sure which was killing him more, pneumonia or restlessness. He breathed oxygen into his nostrils through a clear plastic tube hooked to a droning machine. When he moved about the house, the tube trailed behind him like a strange and awful umbilical cord. He still woke before dawn, and he and Grandma and I would eat breakfast together: oatmeal or eggs or pancakes. Out the window of the kitchen door, in the dim porch light, the large circular thermometer hanging on the tree would read

−20 or −7 or 2 or 11. I would finish breakfast quickly and walk to the store alone.

In the early days of Tremewan's Store, Mel and Gramps talked away whole afternoons while the store sat mostly empty, with steady business coming only an hour or so before the close of each day. There were times when, if someone bought a can of soup, one of them would go back to the warehouse and replace it, right then, even though several more were still left on the shelf. The store didn't break even for the first several years, and so they took any extra work they could. They took odd jobs carpentering. They alternated mornings and afternoons driving the school bus back and forth to Owyhee. Gramps became the head of Sewer and Water. Mel was chief of the Volunteer Fire Department.

There is a story from that time about Gramps and the old International truck which they used to haul produce back from Boise. Mel always tells this story.

"It used to be that Associated Food wouldn't come to Mountain City because we were so small and off its main route. So, once every week, one of us would drive the International four hours to Boise to get fresh fruits and vegetables, leaving by four a.m. so to be back by early afternoon. One of these mornings, Gramps was driving the truck back from Boise, loaded up with produce. Now, Gramps, even back then, was no spring chicken. And you know how old people get. So this particular morning, Gramps falls asleep at the wheel. Ain't that right, Gramps?"

"Like I was in my own bed."

"That old International starts wobbling all over the highway and Gramps wakes up. Seeing that he was about to run off the road, he grabs the wheel and jerks it the opposite way. The truck tips up on its driver side wheels and heads down the highway, then rocks back on all fours and tips the other way, on its passenger side wheels. Finally, it comes down on all fours and heads for home like nothing's happened. Then a highway patrolman pulls Gramps over. Tell them what the man said, Gramps."

"He said he ought to give me a ticket for being all over the road, but it was the damnedest piece of driving he'd ever seen. He said that anybody who could handle a truck like that deserves a medal, not a ticket. He said it would've been perfect except I lost a few head of lettuce on one of the upswings."

I've heard Mel tell this story many times, each time deferring to Gramps just at the end, letting him finish the story, like it was his, like it was something he would have told anyone.

Off the highway, back against the river, the old courthouse and jail stand boarded up and ironic since being condemned in 1972. The jail has only two small cells, and back when it was in use, the deputy sheriff kept his office next door in the courthouse, leaving prisoners alone in the jail, unobserved, for long stretches at a time. One cold winter night the flue in the chimney of the jail got clogged somehow, and two men suffocated while the deputy sheriff and the rest of Mountain City slept.

Now, court is held in a climate-controlled double-wide trailer on the hill behind Tremewan's Store. In 1978, after Gramps was elected justice of the peace of the Mountain City Township, he "retired" from the store—which meant that he still went to work every day, but Tremewan's Store was now fully owned by Lou and Mel. Gramps figured there was a conflict of interest if he was sentencing drunk drivers to jail in a court-house a block from where they'd bought liquor in his store.

Just after dawn one day in April, I woke startled to the report of a gun. The crack was loud and close. Out my window, I saw Gramps walking slowly back to the garage, his rifle in his hands. The shot's echo hung suspended over the meadow and the river and the hills behind my grandparents' place. Then the quiet returned. The wind swirled in the bare branches of the aspens that line the meadow, and the smell of sage swirled with it and was unmistakable and everywhere.

I watched him as he walked from the garage to the house. He walked purposefully, resolved, as though something had just been done that needed doing and now was over. His face was red from wind, his white hair was uncombed, and he hadn't yet shaved. It was a cold morning, and except for boots and jeans, he wore only his gray long-underwear top. Without the heavy, zip-pered sweatshirt he usually wore, I could see how much he'd thinned from the winter's pneumonia, and I thought then that Grandma shouldn't have let him outside like that. I thought also that Gramps should have known better, but didn't. And I wasn't used to thinking of him that way.

That Gramps's body was failing him was something I'd accepted. But I had never before questioned his judgment. That spring, I found myself thinking that there were things that Gramps shouldn't be allowed to do, as if now there were deci-sions he could no longer make for himself.

Gramps's eyes had been going bad for some time, a year or more. Macular degeneration, the doctors called it. It wasn't blindness. It wasn't that simple. He could still see. But he could see well only peripherally, out the corners of his eyes, and, as justice of the peace, Gramps was not a man accustomed to looking at life sideways. His beliefs were simple and uncomplicated. He loved the truth and hated lies, and he believed in accountability, in owning up to responsibilities. He was uncomfortable talking about his own weakness, and the pneumonia and loss of vision had silenced him more. In this way he was typical of the men in the area, a man nearly incapable of asking for help.

But that spring, I'd had to tie his fisherman's knots for him; he could no longer thread a hook's eye. When he went into the garage in midday, the abrupt change from light to dark blinded him. Inside, he felt around with his hands for the things he wanted. He knew his tools, knew where he kept them, and would not wait for his eyes to adjust. Coming out into bright sunlight, he would stand fixed in the yard for seconds, frustrated, unable to gain his bearings, his blue eyes as dim and muddied as floodwater.

At breakfast, I asked Gramps about the shot.

"Got that coyote that'd been hanging around the meadow," he answered, between bites of fried eggs and toast. "Seen it down there for days, moving in and out of the willows by the river. Connolley's letting his cattle out tomorrow."

Jim Connolley lived just outside town, and this time of year he ran his cattle on the meadow behind my grandparents' place. Spring was calving season, and Gramps, having been raised on a ranch, had seen what coyotes could do to newborn calves.

"Did you kill it?" I asked.

"It went down," he said.

I couldn't remember the last time Gramps had fired a gun. And I wouldn't have thought he could hit a coyote, even with the rifle's high-powered scope. From across the table, I studied him the way one studies a clock whose ability to keep time is in doubt, its internal mechanisms hidden. I wanted to know if, for even a moment, he questioned his decision that morning. Not the decision to kill a coyote, for that wouldn't be something he'd consider. What I wanted to know was whether he questioned the wisdom of firing a gun at all, at anything. I wanted to tell him that I was wondering these things. And I wondered if that was something I could bring myself to do.

After breakfast, Gramps and I walked the quarter mile down the highway to the store. We were quiet and walked without speaking. Above the town, the water tower cast its dark silhouette against the hillside, warmed yellow by the sun's low angle. Below, Mountain City waited in shadow: the old schoolhouse, the few houses and buildings whose lights had already been or would soon be turned on, the Miner's Club, the store. The highway was empty. In the two-hundred-mile stretch of road between Elko and Mountain Home, Idaho, in the middle of which sat Mountain City, we knew that at this hour few cars were traveling, and the sense of this magnified the quiet inside us.

Except for a single light above the meat counter, where Mel would be going over the books from the day before, the store was dark. We turned on the light switches and waited for the first customer to arrive. Despite wool socks and boots, we felt the chill rising up through the floorboards, and we stamped our feet and kept moving. Gramps swept. I brought ice up from the back to stock the bins of soda bottles. The old heater in the center of the store knocked and clicked and awakened slowly.

Mel strolled up the center aisle to the front. "Which one of you two shot the river this morning? Was that you, Gramps?"

"No cause to shoot the river," Gramps said.

"Gramps shot the town coyote," I said. In Mountain City, a few people, like Mel and myself, had sympathy for coyotes, and when a coyote was shot near town, we called it the town coyote.

Mel smiled. "Gramps, you oughta know better. Lot of people around here were fond of that coyote."

"If he'd agree not to take them calves, I'd let him go," Gramps said. "But you can't keep a coyote under contract."

"You sure you got him? Sounded like I heard a splash after that shot."

"I got him," Gramps said gruffly.

"I've heard that one before. Remember that pack rat out at the Stump Creek cabin?" Mel sat up on the counter. "One time, Gramps and I were in our bunks with the lantern out, and I was about half asleep when Gramps said, 'Mel, are you in your bed?' and I said, 'Yeah, what for?' and then *boom!* I about hit the ceiling. Gramps had a shotgun beside the bed and he shot the hell out of the woodpile. Wood chips were everywhere. And I said, 'What the hell you do that for?' And he said, 'We got a pack rat. Listen. Let's see if I got the sonofabitch.' And the cabin's quiet for a minute, and then we hear the scurrying and Gramps said, 'Damn!' and then *boom!* He blows into the woodpile again."

"Never did get that pack rat," Gramps said, grinning.

"No, you didn't," Mel retorted. "Which is why I thought of him in connection with our coyote."

Mel loved telling stories about Gramps which portrayed him

in a comic light. It was the side of Gramps that few people knew well, the side that came out rarely as his eyes and health deteriorated and he retreated inside himself.

The day passed slowly. Out the front window of the store the air was damp and cool and gray. Around noon, Gramps went home to have lunch with Grandma and take his nap. Later that afternoon, Lee Chambers, Rosella's son, came in the store asking if anyone had seen his dog, Fritz. Lee hadn't seen him since early that morning.

Lee had been raised in Mountain City and never left. He was near sixty, divorced, and when he wasn't away working in the mines, he lived with Rosella in her trailer home a few blocks up the hill from the store. More than thirty years earlier, Lee and my mother had been sweethearts, and once Lee had asked her to marry him. She'd said no, and then she'd left Mountain City shortly afterwards. There was a sadness to Lee which I always felt strangely a part of, as if I were the reminder of what had never been.

Lee and Fritz were nearly inseparable. The dog napped on the front of Lee's pickup as he drove around town, the best hood ornament in Elko County. Fritz could take corners in his sleep.

"I haven't seen him," said Mel.

"That's not like him to run off," I said.

"I wonder where the hell he's gone," said Lee.

"I hate to suggest it," said Mel, "but a good-looking dog like that, maybe somebody stopped and picked him up and drove off with him. Fritz sure is friendly enough." And then Mel paused, like he'd thought of something else.

"What's that?" Lee asked.

"Nothing. . . . I was just trying to think who'd want to take that dog. I wouldn't want to accuse anybody."

Mel looked over at me quickly, a look Lee didn't catch. Then it occurred to me. Fritz was a malamute, a big dog, bigger than any coyote, and unwary, something Gramps might be able to see.

"God, I hope nobody took him," Lee said.

Mel and I were quiet.

"Okay. Thanks then," Lee said. "I'm gonna keep asking around."

Mel waited for the door to close behind Lee, then motioned to me with his head and walked to the kitchen in the back of the store. I followed. Mel sat down at the table. We ate lunch at this table, and it was stacked high with old newspapers, two bags of opened potato chips, half of a loaf of bread, a near empty jar of mayonnaise, and a knife. I leaned against the doorframe. Mel was looking away to the shelves of shoe boxes that covered the wall opposite the table. He looked as if he were searching for some answer among the different brands and sizes of shoes. His shoulders slumped and he looked weary.

"You figuring what I'm figuring?"

I nodded my head. "You think that was Fritz he shot this morning?"

"Nobody took that dog." Mel went on, "What I can't figure is how he could've hit the damn thing. I wouldn't take a bet he could hit an elephant. But that old bastard's cagey. You can't tell what he sees or can't see."

"He hadn't shot that gun in a long time," I said.

"That's part of it," Mel said. And then his voice slowed, and it grew louder as he spoke. "Gramps knows he's slipping and he's fighting it. If there's a coyote in that meadow, and Connolley's running calves out there tomorrow, Gramps has got to do something. If he doesn't then he might as well hang her up. He's got to shoot it or try to shoot it or he won't know who he is anymore."

Mel looked away from the shoes, and then he looked up, as if he'd heard his voice echo through the small room and come back to him.

"I don't know what to do," he said.

"I know what the right thing to do is," I said.

"Yeah, and what good's that gonna do? That dog's dead," Mel said, fierceness replacing the quiet and the sadness that had been coming on. "I can see what'll happen. Gramps will be sorry as hell and he'll apologize to Lee. And Lee will be sore as hell but won't show it, not to Gramps, not to a man he's looked up to since he was a snot-nosed kid. Gramps will take it like a man, or he'll act like it anyway, but he'll doubt himself more now than he ever did this winter. And you know what else?"

Mel was practically yelling now, but not at me. He was yelling at the situation, at the choice we were facing.

"People are gonna hear about it and think it's funny. The old man thinks he's shooting a coyote and ends up shooting the neighbor's dog. People are gonna come in here, and they're gonna want to laugh. And I won't think it's funny, but I'm gonna have to hide that, cause I can't blame them for thinking that way. They don't know Gramps like I do. And what if Gramps hears them talking or laughing or even senses people are laughing at him? How's he gonna take that?"

Mel stood up, and now everything about his posture suggested decision.

"I say the hell with right and wrong."

"That's not what he'd want," I said.

"I know it, but hell, what he'll never know won't hurt him."

"That's not true for Lee. He's just going to keep looking. He loved that dog."

"Maybe that's something we're both gonna have to live with."

For a minute or so neither of us spoke. Mel looked back to the shoes as if for confirmation. He ran his finger along the edge of a shelf, displacing a thin cloud of dust. He looked at me again as if he intended to speak, and then looked away, down from the shoes to the worn tile of the kitchen floor. And I knew then that Mel would never tell this story to anyone. He would never expose Gramps as a fool. And I knew also that this untold story would color and constrain every future story told, and that right then, as Mel sank back into his chair, spent and heartsick, something irretrievable had been lost.

I left Mel there in the kitchen and walked down the store's center aisle and on out the front door, onto the roadside, where a diesel truck pulling a horse trailer was shifting from a lower gear to a higher one and easing its way up the highway and out of town, past the Forest Service building, past Mel and Lou's, and past my grandparents' place, where they would be preparing the night's dinner for all of us. Grandma peeling potatoes. Gramps stirring the gravy, his oxygen cord coiled in his free hand like a rawhide rope.

At the edge of the meadow beside the river, I found Fritz's body. It was neither warm nor cold. There was little blood; the bullet had passed through its spine. The dry yellow ryegrass was matted flat where it had fallen. Standing over the dead dog, I thought back to the morning and the gunshot and my waking to its noise. I hadn't thought then that the sound could signal the end of anything.

For the first time in my life, I pitied my grandfather, though I couldn't have named the feeling then, for it was the one feeling I thought I'd never have for him. Never pity. He could not see the terms that old age had given him, terms that I, barely a man by comparison in years and things seen, could see clearly. And I resented this blindness, and I resented the dog at my feet, which I should have pitied but couldn't, not until much later. And I resented Gramps for killing a thing that meant so much to one man and so little to me, so that my choice then could not be balanced or fair or just, which was all I wanted. The same things Gramps wanted. I knew those things. And I knew what Gramps would have done, had he been me.

In the sky above the meadow, streaks of copper were fading into coal and iron, and dark was coming on. I dragged Fritz's body down the five-foot bank and dumped it in the river.

It is just after five, the busiest time of day for the store, and my cousin Graham and I are at the front ringing up customers. I'm running the register, and Graham is bagging groceries. He's good help. He knows to set the heavy cans and jars at the bottom, the produce in a separate plastic bag, the bread and paper towels on top. He knows not to bag the gallon jugs of milk.

Graham is twenty-five, a few years younger than me. He's come to visit for a few weeks from his home in Cedar City, Utah. He's almost six feet tall, and his two hundred and twenty pounds hang loosely on an unmuscled frame which moves sluggishly, awkwardly, as if unbalanced or overburdened. His eyes are dark and brown and open and his face is smooth, with only a few traces of hair. Graham almost always wears a plaid flannel shirt, like Gramps, and he's wearing it now, in June. He's wearing his green apron also, like the rest of us.

Graham has had leukemia since he was three. He's one of the longest-surviving leukemia patients in the country. But the side effects of all the years of experimentation and blind groping for cures, of all the chemotherapy and radiation, caused seizures that killed brain cells. With each seizure, Graham's mind suffered and retreated. His cancer has been in remission for years, but he still fades in and out of health, plagued by the unpredictable seizures. During the bad times, Graham can lose a hundred pounds in a few months. It's happened more times than I can remember.

Graham and I grew up together. We spent our summers here in Mountain City, playing and working in the store, exploring the town and the river and the hills. As adults, we both keep coming back, for more or less the same reason. We don't feel as whole anywhere else.

Carrying a bag of groceries under each arm, Graham follows Rosella out the front door to her car. One at a time, she takes a bag from Graham and sets it in the trunk. Then, placing her hand on Graham's back, she walks him up the steps to the front door.

"Thank you, dear," she says.

Graham doesn't respond. He opens the door and comes back over beside me and resumes his responsibilities, placing a six-pack of soda at the bottom of a new paper bag.

Only in a place like Mountain City could Graham do this. He is slow, inefficient. You have to watch him, help him. He could never do this in a city. In a supermarket, with the thousands of people a day rushing through the store, some customers might be patient and understand, but many would not. They would grumble or complain outright. For the people of Mountain City, it's not a matter of waiting or not waiting. They ask Graham questions.

"What's new, Graham?" says Larry Monroe. Larry was born and raised in Elko County, left as a young man, and came back after years of commercial fishing up in Alaska. He looks the part. He has a thick, dark beard and a midsection to be proud of. He is almost as big as Graham.

"*I* flew the *air*plane," Graham says.

"You did?"

"I *did*." Graham's voice is muffled, blurry, and his words are difficult to distinguish unless you're used to the pattern of his speech. Larry's used to it.

"You're a pilot?"

"*I* flew the *air*plane!"

Graham's father, my uncle Paul, was once a pilot and used to take Graham with him sometimes when he flew. Graham hasn't been in the cockpit of a plane for years, but it's one of his imagination's favorite places.

"Where'd you go?" Larry asks.

"*I* flew the plane to Salt *Lake!*"

There is something poetic about Graham's speech. He has neither a child's nor an adult's inflections. The emphasis he places on particular words is, to me, surprising and wonderful. He loves the engagement of conversation. When he talks, he rubs his hands together excitedly. But he's often silent unless you first ask him a question. If you told Graham to reshelve a can of peaches, he might look up, his brown eyes no longer a vacant field of clay, and he might take and reshelve the can. Or he might stare out the front window. But if you say, "Graham, do you know where *this* goes? Will you show me?" He will take you to the spot, to the middle of the third aisle, on the bottom shelf.

———

When Graham bags groceries at Tremewan's Store, he won't bag cigarettes. It's not simply that he prefers not to, like Melville's Bartleby. It's more than that. He sermonizes. Graham is a Mormon, two of his older sisters are nurses, and having been through so much hospitalization himself, Graham is health conscious. When someone places a pack of cigarettes on the counter, Graham says, "Cigarettes *kill* you." He sometimes says this a few times, for emphasis. And then he won't put them in a bag.

When Mel or Lou works the register and Graham says this, everyone usually laughs, and then Mel or Lou bags the cigarettes for the customer. When Graham bags for me, I won't bag the cigarettes either. I won't undermine his authority. Nobody needs to listen to me about health and how to live, but everybody could stand to listen to Graham.

Graham calls his mom and dad by their first names, Paul and Di. When he's around strangers, Graham calls his parents by their full names, Paul Graff and Diana Graff. They've taught him to do this so that if he ever gets lost, someone will be able to help him.

When Graham comes to Mountain City, he goes wherever he wants and keeps his own schedule. This is the only place he's allowed to do this, and so I think Mountain City is Graham's place more than Grandma's or Gramps's or Rosella's or any one of the thirty-three people who live here. The stakes are higher for Graham. The privileges are greater. If Graham takes his time crossing the highway, no one honks or swerves around him.

They stop and wait. They lean out the window and ask him what he's up to, where he's headed. If he's playing in Bobbie Culley's flower bed, which he likes to do, she brings out an extra spade and they put in rhododendrons. Graham wanders all over town: up the rutted dirt road to the old schoolhouse, down along the Owyhee, where he talks to the cows on the opposite bank, up through sagebrush to the water tower, which overlooks the town and the river and the meadows. He does the same things that he and I used to do together when we were kids. Now, sometimes, I accompany him on his travels around town. It's not that different.

Grandma, Di, Lou, and I are playing hearts. It's late, past eleven, and we've been playing for hours, sitting around my grandparents' kitchen table. Graham is sitting at the table with us, playing his own game with his own deck of cards. His game goes like this: He takes the top card from the deck, studies it, and then places it in one of five piles. Each suit has its own pile. The fifth pile is for aces and face cards, which all go together, regardless of their suit. Graham plays the game until all the cards are in their respective piles, and then he pushes the piles together and plays again. He doesn't need to shuffle. The game is new every time.

Within the basic framework of the game, there are many subtleties. When the number eight appears, Graham holds out the card and says, "*That's* an eight. *That's* when Gramps goes to *bed.*" Graham is right and knows it, and he laughs and smiles and rubs his hands together. And Grandma says, "That's right,

Graham. That *is* an eight. That's when Gramps goes to bed."
This makes Graham even happier. Meanwhile, Gramps, who is
sleeping in the next room, sleeps on. Graham takes another card.

"*That's* a seven. *That's* when Gianna goes to *work.*" Gianna is
Graham's older sister. She's a nurse in Cedar City and works
twelve-hour night shifts. Sometimes Graham says, "*That's* a
seven. *That's* when Gianna gets off work." It's one of the game's
options.

"*That's* a six. *That's* when Sky West lands in *Salt* Lake."

Not all of the numbers have corresponding pronouncements. I've never heard Graham say anything about the numbers
two, or four, or nine. Sometimes Graham draws the number six
or seven or eight and says nothing. Sometimes Graham holds up
a card and just stares at it quietly, holding it up for some time.

"That's a ten, Graham," Lou says. "That's when the news
comes on."

Sometimes this will prompt Graham, and he will repeat the
phrase back to us, remembering it the way an elderly person
might remember a childhood friend, suddenly, fondly. Other
times, Graham looks into the card and through it, as if it has
triggered something deep inside himself, something he can't
possibly articulate with a number or the time of day. Sometimes
we'll take the card from his hand, place it in its pile, wipe the
drool from his face, and hope the game will go on. Most often
it does.

Graham has nothing to say about face cards or aces. They're a
mystery. I don't know why Graham doesn't arrange them by suit
also. Perhaps this is the point where Graham's mind comes up
against its limitations. Or perhaps he simply doesn't want to

arrange the face cards by suit. Perhaps it's because he feels that face cards and aces are all of equal importance. Perhaps it's because he doesn't think they are nearly as important as the numbered cards. It's impossible to know. But I do know this: in Graham's own way, the game is highly refined. It is a system. It is a game, and it is not a game. It is one of his ways of making sense of the world, of putting things in their place.

When Graham and I come to Mountain City, we're the only men in town in our twenties. Mountain City's widows, Margaret and Rosella and Bobbie and Dorothy, refer to us as the bachelors. "Well if it isn't the bachelors, back again," Rosella says, coming into the store one summer day. "Hold on to your belt buckles."

"Afternoon, Rosella," I say.

"Get *out* of the way! You're *blocking* the *door!*" says Graham, and then he starts laughing so hard he almost falls off the counter he's sitting on.

"Don't you *John Wayne* me, Graham Graff," says Rosella. "I've handled more than a few cowboys in my day, and I can handle one more."

Graham laughs even harder and rubs his hands together. Graham's hero is John Wayne, and this line of his comes from *Hondo,* a movie Graham has seen more times than most people would think possible. Graham does his John Wayne impression whenever anyone stands in the doorway with the door open for more than a moment, which is pretty often.

When Graham doesn't get his way, his refusals are creative. It's the middle of July, and he and Di are going home to Cedar City tomorrow. But Graham doesn't want to leave Mountain City, so he's crossed out tomorrow and the next day and the next on the calendar at Tremewan's Store. He's got all the days marked off halfway into August. His work starts again in the middle of August, and Graham likes work, so he's willing to go home for that. Each weekday from nine to five Graham works at a supervised shop with other adults like him. He builds wooden pallets used in the freight industry. After work my uncle Paul picks Graham up, and they drive to the airport and watch Sky West's 5:15 flight to Salt Lake taxi down the runway and take off.

Fifteen miles east of Mountain City, there's a ghost town named after our great-great-great-uncle. The town's name is, or was, Rowland, after Gramps's great-uncle Rowland Gill, his grandmother's brother, a miner from Cornwall who became a rancher, who settled the area in the late nineteenth century. There's nothing there now but a few caved-in mine shafts, some house-shaped depressions in the earth, and the remains of a chimney.

Graham doesn't know his family history. He doesn't know any history. He doesn't know that Gramps's full name is Oliver Rowland Tremewan. Graham knows his older brother's name is Rowland Graff, but he can't associate a name with a reason or a history or a place. He can't understand that being a Tremewan descendant in northern Elko County, Nevada, is a bit like being a *Mayflower* descendant in Massachusetts. He can tell you that he's "pioneer stock," and he will, if you ask him. But he doesn't know what that means. Graham can't tell you that this country is in his blood. He can't tell you that he belongs here, but he does, and he knows he does. He just can't tell you.

Graham is gently shaken awake by Di's hand at his shoulder. His eyes open slowly, and it is some time before he sits up and orients himself in his world. He wakes always like this, emerging each morning from sleep like a bear from winter. He can't rise from sleep with expectation. He can't wake excited or anxious or hesitant. Whatever anticipation he may have harbored at bedtime has been lost in dream or the spaces between dreams, and he wakes blank, like an amnesiac who must be told his name.

Graham takes a shower and dresses himself in the clothes Di has set out for him. Once dressed, Graham puts on his coat, hat, and gloves and goes out the back door into the cold morning. It's winter, and Graham and Di have come to Mountain City for a few weeks over Christmas. It has snowed two inches during the night, and Graham starts the snowblower and begins clearing the driveway. No one has asked him to do this. He's fully awake now, and the chain of events that make his life has been set in motion. He's happy. It shows on his face through the fog of his breath. He pushes the machine in front of him and powder flies out its side onto a low berm of old crusted snow at the driveway's edge. Graham calls this "cutting the snow." In the summer, when Graham comes to Mountain City, he cuts our grandparents' grass every single morning. In the summer, they have the best-kept yard in town.

Graham has cleared most of the driveway when the small engine of the blower falters and stops and the white morning goes quiet. Graham stoops down, rests one knee on the bare pavement, and unscrews the cap to the engine's tank. He peers down and sees that it's empty.

Graham goes to the dark garage, to the back right corner, finds the can of gas, lifts it, and carries it and a funnel out to the blower. When Graham lifts the can of gas, he doesn't stop to gauge its weight, to see how full it is, to see whether there's enough gas to fill the tank. There's always enough gas. Gramps keeps it full; not to do so would extend the chain of decision and action beyond Graham's capacity. For twenty-five years, our family has gauged this capacity.

Graham fills the tank, screws the lid back in place, and returns the gas can and funnel to their places in the garage. He starts the blower again, finishes the driveway, and clears the sidewalk. Inside the house, he finds Gramps waiting for him, with a breakfast of eggs and bacon on the table. After breakfast, the two men walk the quarter mile down the highway to the store.

My grandparents have an old home movie from back when Graham and I were kids. I haven't seen it in years, but I remember it vividly. We're all gathered in our grandparents' living room, and Graham and I and our brothers and sisters and cousins are giving a sort of talent show, performing skits and singing songs. Graham and I are both dressed in our cowboy outfits: boots, spurs, Stetsons, Western shirts, belt buckles, the works. I'm singing "The Gambler," by Kenny Rogers, and I'm fumbling, forgetting the words. In the background my family is singing the words to me, helping me along. You can hear Graham's voice too, so distinct even back then. "Know when to walk away, know when to run." Then Graham's singing his song, "Rhinestone Cowboy." And he's singing loudly and clearly and pointing his finger to different people in the crowd as he sings, at Grandma, Aunt Lou, my mom, Uncle Mel. He's hamming it up. He knows every word.

Gramps, Mel, and I sit up front on the counters. It's morning, and the store is empty. The day before, Graham had a seizure and collapsed in the center aisle, striking his head on the hardwood floor. He lay there without moving for what seemed a long time, until Mel rushed over, knelt down, and put a hand on his shoulder. Graham muttered something then, but didn't cry or wail the way a child might. He just looked up at Mel, unsurprised, uncomprehending. He hadn't suffered a seizure in weeks.

"His eyes were as empty as I've ever seen them," Mel says. "Like the fall knocked him clear back to zero. For a minute there, before I saw his eyes, I thought to myself, Oh God, we've lost him."

No one says anything for some time. Gramps's eyes, too, are empty, a milked blue, and they stare ahead fiercely, at nothing. His hands grip the counter firmly. Then he says, "My brother Syd's boy was the same as Graham. Worse. Every day there was the worry he'd die. The boy lived to be near thirty. Every day there was that fear. Syd should've let that boy die when he was born."

Then Gramps hesitates, as if about to say the next thing, to complete the analogy. But he doesn't. He doesn't believe that. He lowers his head and looks down at the floor. For Gramps, silence is the fence he builds to hold in the things he knows. When Graham comes to visit, he spends most of his time with Gramps, working in the yard, sitting with him on the front counter at the store, the two of them quiet or Graham telling Gramps about the plane to Salt Lake. I wonder if Gramps's feelings for Graham now are a reflection of his own fear, as if Graham were a mirror in which Gramps sees himself in the time to come: blind, dependent, invalided. After a long while, Gramps goes to the back, gets his sweatshirt, and walks home.

Graham comes in the front door of the store wearing light blue scrubs which read: PLAINVIEW MEDICAL CENTER. He's carrying a clipboard, and when Mel sees him, Mel says loudly, for everyone to hear, "The doctor is *in!*"

Graham shouts back, "*I'm* Dr. Graff!" and then he goes over to Mel and starts scribbling furiously on the Tremewan's Store credit slip he has attached to his clipboard.

"Doc, am I gonna make it?" Mel asks.

"*I* think so," Graham says, and then he hands Mel the slip, which is entirely illegible and looks a lot like a doctor's prescription. "*Three* times a *day,*" Graham says.

We haven't seen Graham in a while. He's been spending a lot of time in the hospital lately, making his rounds.

When Dr. Graff bags groceries at Tremewan's Store, he doesn't wear a green apron. "*Doctors* don't wear green aprons," he says.

The Associated Food truck has come and gone, and the boxes are stacked in rows by the warehouse door. All morning I've been emptying them onto storage shelves: pickles, cereal, pork and beans, catsup, peanut butter—a long list of things. Most all of this will go out front and eventually feed this small section of Elko County. Those few items that remain won't leave this back room, won't pay for themselves, leading a shelf life all their own.

The empty boxes get tossed in a haphazard pile over by the deep freeze. We'll use these for packing when paper or plastic won't do, for hauling groceries in the beds of pickups. Graham comes back to the warehouse to help me, and we throw the empty boxes on the pile.

"Graham, do *you* think so?" I ask him, in reference to nothing particular.

"*I* think so!" he answers, smiling. I don't know why, but he loves this question, so I ask it often.

I didn't tell Graham that the boxes didn't need to be stacked, to be placed carefully, like the eggs he handles gently when he's up front bagging, like the way he's been handled his whole life. He could see for himself the lack of order, of care. He just started chucking them on the pile, box after box, with different spins, arcs, and motions, pausing, after each toss, to rub his hands together excitedly, his sign for happiness, for joy.

Rosella lies on the cold concrete floor of her garage. Her hip is broken, the bone snapping cleanly, easily, like a thistle reed in the hands of a small child. It's winter and there's ice in the garage, but Rosella didn't slip on the ice. She stepped down the one step from her back door onto the garage floor. The one step. Her thin weight shifted and its demand on bone could not be met. Then she fell.

A few weeks before, without explanation, Rosella stopped going to coffee in the morning at the Miner's Club with the widows. Without her, Bobbie and Margaret and Dorothy felt lost and incomplete. They were somber and sullen, and this feeling traveled through the wall to Tremewan's Store, and Mel stopped singing his show tunes and instead hummed them to himself dolefully.

For as long as I could remember, Rosella had come to the store every day, usually after meeting with the widows next door. But lately she'd been coming less frequently. A few times a week. Twice a week. Lee had gone to work for a mine several hours away and was home now only a couple weekends each month. When Lou asked Rosella where she'd been hiding lately, Rosella said she didn't need many groceries these days.

Rosella didn't weigh ninety pounds, but lately, impossibly, she looked like she'd been losing weight. She looked pale and sickly; her complexion, the skin on her arms, even her red hair seemed drained of color. And so we wondered then, each of us, at Tremewan's Store, at the Miner's Club, at the Post Office and Reed's Service Station, we wondered if Rosella was able to take care of herself anymore. We wondered if she might be better off in Elko, in the nursing home, where someone would look after her each day. We did not want that, any of us, and we knew Rosella didn't either. She had lived in Mountain City most of her life and didn't intend on leaving now. But we wondered.

After a couple weeks of this, Lou decided something had to be done. So each day around noon, I walked a bag of groceries up the hill to Rosella's house, and we had lunch together. Most often we ate soup. Rosella rarely finished her bowl.

"You've got to eat, Rosella," I said one day. "You're too thin. You don't have anything left to lose."

"I know it," she said.

"Then why don't you?"

"I'm not hungry anymore."

This way of talking, this clipped and abbreviated speech, was not like us. Rosella was never a talker, like Mel, but she wasn't quiet either. Her trips to the store, like most people's in town, were as much for visiting as for buying groceries. She sometimes stayed an hour, chatting up front at the registers. *What did the paper say today? How are you feeling this morning, Oliver? How long will you be with us this time, Gregory?*

But sitting across from each other at her kitchen table, we hardly spoke. I wanted to joke with her, to make her laugh, but couldn't. Her flowered blouse hung from her shoulders as if from wire. We each, separately, looked out the window to the few inches of snow on the ground, to the schoolhouse on the hill, its windows boarded, its playground swings with only the cold wind to give them purpose.

Rosella lies on the concrete floor of her garage, her hip is broken, and she's alone. She doesn't cry out or cry. She lives on a hill four blocks up from town and two blocks from the nearest neighbor, and she couldn't make her voice reach that far if she wanted to. And she doesn't. She doesn't cry out or cry because she is ninety-one and knows those things do no good.

Riley Chambers, Rosella's husband, has been dead twelve years. Two years before he died, Riley suffered a massive stroke in the car one day on the way to Elko. Rosella was driving. It was forty miles to the hospital. She got him there in twenty-five minutes. When she learned the condition he'd be in for the rest of his life, she wished she'd taken an hour.

For two years, Riley sat in a wheelchair in a nursing home in Elko, his eyes vacant, his body listless. Rosella would go to visit him in the big open room there, and the windows would be opened and the blinds pulled up, letting in the air and light of day. And there they'd all be, wheelchairs sitting in every direction.

Riley had been a rancher all his life and wouldn't have wanted it that way, and Rosella knew it. But there was nothing she could do. There was no plug to pull. If you fed him, he lived. So she did what everyone else in Mountain City was doing then. She prayed for him to die.

The image of Riley that Rosella wishes she could hold in her mind is of the time before the stroke. It's summer and it's dusk and he's just come in the house from haying, dusty and sweat soaked, and he's leaning into the kitchen doorframe. His faded red cap is in his hand and his thin yellow hair is matted wet and dark and flat on his head. He is not at all young, but standing there, he is tall and healthy and all that he once was.

Most people don't get to choose how or where or when to die. The ones who do are lucky. Rosella's hip is broken, and she's thinking of being found on the concrete floor of her garage, cold and alive. She's thinking of Riley sitting in his wheelchair. She's thinking of that big open room. She's thinking, *No. Not if I can help it.*

———

A broom leans into the corner of the garage. Rosella rolls over onto what is now her good side and with her hands and elbows and forearms she scrapes her way along the concrete to the broom. Reaching it, she rests and breathes deeply and her chest and ribs and the lungs they veil thinly expand and contract and expel air as white as ghosts.

Pushing the broom ahead of her, Rosella drags herself back to her Jeep. She rests again. Bracing the broom against the car, leaning into it, she reaches up and opens the driver's door. The Jeep's running board is two feet above the concrete floor. Now with the broom against the running board, she pushes her thin body up and reaches for the steering wheel. Grasping it, she pulls herself into the seat. She rests a moment. The Jeep is an automatic, thank God, and Lee has the idle set high, so all she has to do is turn the key that never leaves the ignition and put her in gear. She does this, backs out of the garage, and drives the four blocks to town.

She parks the Jeep in front of Tremewan's Store and honks the horn, once.

After a minute or so, Lou comes out, and Rosella rolls down the window.

"Morning, Rosella," Lou says. She's a bit puzzled because Rosella has never before demanded drive-up service.

"Hi, Lou," Rosella says, then pauses. "Listen, Lou, if it's not too much trouble, could you drive me to Elko? My hip's broken."

Tremewan's Store is cold and dark as Mel and I turn on the light switches and get ready to open. Gramps opens the cupboards above the coffeemaker, feels for where the filters should be, the can of Hills Bros.

Mel gets the cash from the safe in the back and turns on the front registers. I sweep the floors. Lou will be in soon to stock produce. It's Monday, and my cousin Mitch has gone to Elko for bread and milk. Around ten, an old Basco man comes in. He wears a cowboy hat, a Western shirt, jeans and boots.

"Morning, Oliver," he says.

"Morning," Gramps says.

"Haven't been through in some time. Who's the boy?" The man nods at me in my green apron. With some of these old-timers, *boy* refers to anyone under the age of fifty.

"This is Dolores's boy, Greg," Gramps says.

"Nice to meet you," I say, and we shake hands.

The man steps back, waiting, looking at Gramps as if he expects something from him. He looks confused when, after more than a few moments, it does not come. Gramps looks down at his feet.

"Morning, Frank," Mel says, coming up the main aisle from the back. "This here Basco is Frank Badia," my uncle says to me. "Your mom used to work for him down at the Forest Service when she was your age."

"I was just about to tell him," Frank says, quieter than before.

Frank buys a few things. He and Mel and Gramps talk for a few minutes, and then he leaves.

"I couldn't make out his voice," Gramps says.

"I know it," Mel says.

"I've known that man all my life."

Fred Badia, Frank Badia's brother, ranched up near Charleston, which is on the road to Jarbridge from North Fork. In his last years, Fred developed Alzheimer's. Here was this old, short, still incredibly vital Basco, whose memory had taken on the topography of his face: weathered all to hell, like baked and blistered clay. During that time, Fred would come into Tremewan's Store with his wife, and, immediately upon entering, he'd fix himself on one person, who, for some reason, was usually Mel. He'd go over, vigorously shake Mel's hand, and introduce himself. "Fred Badia," he'd say. "How you doing?"

"Good, Fred," Mel would say. *"Ondo."*

"Ondo," Fred would answer. *"Ondo."* And then he'd scoot around the store with as much energy as a toddler, up and down

the aisles, ahead of his wife, behind her, taking items down from the shelves and putting them in the cart, her taking them out, putting them back.

Mel, like Gramps, has known the Badias all his life. Both Fred and Frank used to run sheep in the same country as Mel's father. During the winters when Mel was a boy, he ate dinner every night with the two Badia brothers at the long table in the Martin Hotel in Winnemucca. He knew their table manners, how quickly or slowly they ate, what their favorite meal was. Fred was left-handed, ate with his right hand, but held his knife in his left hand. He loved applesauce. Fifty years and Mel remembered that: applesauce.

When Fred returned to the front counter with his wife, their cart full of groceries, he'd do the whole thing over again, the whole ritual. Shake Mel's hand. Introduce himself. Then he'd be gone.

"Gero arte," Mel would say. *"Gero arte."*

At dinner, Mel sits beside Gramps at the table. Mel cuts Gramps's meat for him so he won't have to ask. Gramps's plate is a pie plate, so he won't push food off onto the tablecloth. The two men are quiet. Mel is quiet because he's drunk and believes he can hide it. Gramps is quiet because he can hardly see his food, and because Mel is drunk. After dinner, Gramps will sit in his chair. Mel will stumble next door and fall asleep on his couch.

Grandma, Mel, Eddie, and I are playing pinochle one Sunday evening in my grandparents' living room. Gramps sits in his chair. Eddie and I are partners and we've just taken a trick.

"That's all the spades then," Mel says, loudly. He's wearing his Black Velvet T-shirt, the one he sent away for, like a kid with cereal box tops. He's only a little liquored tonight. It's Sunday, our day off from the store, and Mel usually takes it easy.

"*Shut up*, Mel," Eddie says, just as loudly. Eddie's pretty sober tonight, too. *Shut up* is one of his favorite expressions. "You've been table-talking all night, Mel, and we're still cleaning your clock."

Eddie leads a low diamond.

The etiquette in pinochle, as in most card games, prohibits the announcing of previously played cards or the number of cards played or left to be played in a suit. Mel, as Eddie has noted, has been blabbing, breaking all these rules since we sat down to play.

I hadn't given Mel's table talk much thought, dismissing it as whiskey talk, but Mel keeps on talking, and when Eddie is about to say something again, Mel fixes his eyes on Eddie. Eddie says nothing. We keep playing. Then I notice Gramps, leaning slightly forward in his chair.

Gramps loves all card games, but he no longer plays because he can't distinguish suits, numbers, face cards. He's following the game from Mel's pronouncements. He's counting cards.

Some nights after dinner, when Lou has gone back to the store to do her books and Mel has gone home to lie on his couch,

Grandma, Gramps, and I sit in the living room together. I tune the satellite dish to whatever sports might be on, and Gramps listens to the TV in his chair, picturing the game in his head like with a radio, keeping his mind sharp. He breathes his oxygen through his nose, chewing a bit on the slack of plastic tube he has coiled in his lap. Grandma watches the game in her chair and at the same time reads a book or does her quilting. Whenever there's a basketball game on, college or pro, no matter who's playing, Grandma makes the following proclamation: "That Jordan's getting just a bit too big for his britches, if you ask me." And then she goes back to her book or quilting, and her declaration hangs in the air, entirely rhetorical.

When the game is slow or the ending has already been decided, I try to get Gramps to tell me a story. My favorites are the stories about him as a boy out on the Tremewan Ranch. Grandma is always willing to tell stories, to anyone who will listen, but Gramps is different. Some nights all I can pull from him are one- or two-word responses.

One fall night, after having caught a cold the day before by going outside in his shirtsleeves, he told me, "I always was a hard learner. One winter, when the pump handle was frozen stuck, my dad told me, 'Son, don't try to warm the frost off with your tongue. Your brother tried that when he was your age, and it didn't work.' Dad was laughing a bit when he said that, but at the time I didn't know why. So that's just what I did. Licked the handle. Damn near took all the hide off my tongue and lips trying to come unglued. But that wasn't the end of it. Did it again. Metal rail of a wagon wheel. I figured that if you didn't rear back all of a sudden, then you'd thaw off. I was testing that theory out."

When people in Mountain City talk about weather, they say things like, "The weather's picked up a bit in the last hour," and by this they mean eight inches of snow or sixty-mile-per-hour winds. By *weather,* they mean what most people call bad weather. In winter, they say to newcomers, "What brings you up here to the Yukon?"

Mountain City sits just above fifty-six hundred feet, and once every few years, Wildhorse Crossing, eight miles south of town in the canyon, has the day's record low temperature for the entire lower forty-eight states. Sixty below, not counting windchill. "Below the ought," my grandma says, of any weather below zero, as she looks out the back window to the circular thermometer hanging on the tree. Then she goes back to her quilting while Gramps and I eat our breakfast. Cold is cold. And stoic is stoic. My grandmother, unlike Gramps, is an emotional person, but not about the weather. For more than eighty years, she's been taught to believe that, if you live in this part of the country, the weather is hard, but it's not as hard as you are.

All the ranching families that live up the Trail Creek Road—the Connolleys, Bakers, Thompsons, Beiroths, and Otheims—leave their cars parked down beside the highway when the snow gets bad, and they snowmobile from their houses down to the road. Weekdays, their kids snowmobile down to the school bus, the machines' headlights cutting through the morning dark.

When it comes to deciding whether to drive through weather, the people in Mountain City most often decide to go. They go with blankets and sleeping bags and flashlights and shovels. And they go slow. They figure the weather will break sometime. They figure it'll break before they do. They go because the Quilting Society is meeting with the Elko chapter, because of a high school basketball game, because their grandkids have a Christmas play or need to see the doctor, because they want to get home. If they're lucky, they get behind the plow and follow it until it turns around at the maintenance station, halfway between Elko and Mountain City. Then they wait for the next plow, coming from the opposite direction, to turn around and lead them the rest of the way through the storm.

In northern Elko County, in winter, the men who drive the big orange plows for the Nevada Department of Transportation (NDOT) come into Tremewan's Store and bullshit for hours, on the job, when the weather's not up. They stand around the front counters in their heavy orange jumpsuits and listen to Mel tell jokes. When they do this, no one in Mountain City complains about their tax dollars at work. When the weather demands it, the plows run around the clock, and Highway 225 stays open. Once, when Gramps needed to be rushed to Elko in an ambulance coming from Owyhee, Lou got one of the NDOT guys on the radio, and the ambulance followed the plow the entire eighty-four miles. On the open stretch of highway between Elko and Mountain City, you can be fifteen minutes behind the plow and not get through. The wind blows so hard that three-foot drifts reclaim the road in five minutes.

One cold winter morning Lou came in the side door of the store, hung up her heavy winter coat, put on her green apron, and turned on the heater. She took the shovel from behind the soda case and unlocked the front door. The door wouldn't budge. Frozen, she figured. She pushed harder. Nothing. She went out the side door and walked around and then wished she hadn't pushed so hard. During the night, a kitten had frozen itself to the top step of the concrete porch. It leaned against the door, glazed with ice, translucent, like an alabaster statue.

With tiny, quick taps of a paint scraper, Lou worked the kitten loose, like a brick from mortar. One hand under its belly, the other on its back, she picked it up. She couldn't feel its fur. It felt like it could shatter. She didn't know if it was alive, and if it was, she thought it must be closer to death than life. She wondered if it would want to come back. She wondered if she would want to. She didn't know. She thought of a children's story about a girl who found a baby bird fallen from its nest. She thought of walking the kitten out into the sage. She wrapped it in gunnysacks and put it back in the warehouse. If it thawed too quickly, she thought, it would die of shock.

Those who live in the far-off, disinterested cold sometimes develop a certain kind of patience—willful, stubborn—a fierce patience, which is paradoxical, like many true character traits. Lou had this kind of patience, and so did that kitten, because within an hour it was shivering and breathing thin, raspy, determined breaths. Lou shivered too, and then waited, fiercely, for hours, before swaddling the kitten in baby blankets and placing it in my cousin Molly's crib in the kitchen of the store.

The kitten lived. For nineteen years. Lou named her JB, which stood for Just Bones. JB grew up in Tremewan's Store, had many kittens of her own, and proved to be as healthy as any cat there ever was, despite her missing tail, ears, and toes.

My aunt Lou does not dote, not on people, not on animals, not on anything. And she did not dote on JB. She did not pick her up without good reason, or adopt a kittenish tone of voice, the way most people do. She figured that any animal that had the courage and will to return from that much cold deserved a kind of respect that allowed no room for foolishness. If JB was standing by the front door of the store, Lou let her out, or in, without ceremony. When they passed each other in the aisles of Tremewan's Store, Lou would say, "Hello, JB." In good weather, JB came and went as she pleased, rarely staying indoors overnight. In winter, JB slept at the foot of Lou and Mel's bed, and she sat in the passenger seat and drove with Lou down to the store in the mornings and back home in the evenings.

Mel had the good sense to not speak disparagingly of JB. He didn't want to end up frozen to the front porch of Tremewan's Store.

Though JB never wore a green apron, she did do her share of work around the store. She was an accomplished mouser. And she sat on the counter beside Lou when she rang up customers. Sometimes JB would paw at the groceries as Lou set them in the bag. My cousin Graham liked to bag JB, so that the very top of her earless head would emerge strangely from out the top of the sack. Some customers, especially strangers passing through on the highway, found this a bit unnerving.

In winter, brutal winds whip down from the hills, and the cattle in the meadows huddle closely together, their heads sluggish and lowered and turned in the same direction. They do not bawl or make any sound. Once positioned, they hardly move. Snow falls constantly, and in cold sunshine, the country turns a blinding, reflected white. Snowpack and ice cover the highway, and the orange trucks of the state highway department pass by daily with their salt and their rumbling engines and their plows scraping down to the frozen asphalt.

Winter is a time of worry. For me, for Grandma and Gramps, for Mel and Lou and Mitch. Will Gramps come down with pneumonia again? If he does, will this be the winter that kills him? Grandma and Gramps spend most of their time indoors. If he is still healthy, Gramps insists on walking down to the store each morning. And each winter, Gramps catches a cold. His pneumonia is chronic.

One morning in October, when Gramps was sick with bronchitis, my cousin Molly called to ask me if I could come out to the ranch that she and her husband manage and help them with pregnancy checking. I told her I would, and then called Mel to tell him that I wouldn't be coming down to the store that morning.

Grandma was in the kitchen with me, finishing up a quilt she'd been working on for months. The quilt was for Molly's second son, Todd, who was only a few months old. Grandma makes quilts for all her grandchildren and great-grandchildren. She has mended my quilt countless times. I had just set the phone back in its cradle when she started screaming at me.

"You're no goddamn good, you know that." The veins in her neck bulged, and her voice was tight, as if she was trying to funnel all her anger through a tiny opening in her throat.

"Grandma."

"Your word doesn't mean a thing around here."

I hadn't seen it coming. I never did, and I knew I should have left before it got worse, before she said something that would be hard to forget. I had come that fall after college to work in the store, and Grandma thought then, in her rage, that any deviation from that purpose was a form of betrayal. There was always a logic to her anger, no matter how irrational it seemed, but I knew that arguing or trying to explain myself would do no good. Still, I couldn't help myself. I wanted her to take back what she'd said. I wanted to tell her that her condemnation was something I could hardly stand.

"I'm going to help Molly and Justin," I said weakly.

"You're not doing anything for anybody but yourself," she said, shaking her finger wildly. "I know you. You're not fooling anyone."

"Grandma."

"I'm not listening to another goddamn word. Get out of here. Get the hell out."

Grandma didn't talk to me when I came home that night. She wouldn't look at me. The day before, Gramps had been to the hospital in Owyhee. His blood pressure was low. He was coughing all the time and sat covered with a quilt in his chair in the living room. He wouldn't lie down in bed. As long as he could sit up, he would. He had hives also, which we'd been told were the physical manifestation of his own worry and fear. Grandma didn't talk to me for three days.

When Gramps is sick, Grandma's anger is unpredictable, and she directs it outward as precisely as a shotgun blast, at anyone, even at Gramps. If he forgets to take his medicine. If he doesn't have his slippers on his feet. If he stays up later than usual listening to a ball game on television. Grandma's fury rages when any one of us does the things we have always done before, when we do the smallest, most incidental things.

During such times, when we're all gathered around the table for dinner, Mel often says something like "Nobody light a match, or this place is gonna blow." No one ever laughs. Gramps is sick, and we don't know if he'll get better. Grandma is not herself, and we know that she hardly knows it, for she won't apologize later and instead behaves as if nothing has happened. We know that her frantic anxiety will fade only as Gramps's bronchitis or pneumonia fades. And we know also, though we won't say it, that hers is another kind of sickness, brought on by age, and it is a sickness of the mind.

Whenever Lou or Grandma loses her temper, for the next few days the patrons of Tremewan's Store can expect to hear Mel tell this joke:

An Elko man goes to the doctor and learns he has terminal cancer, six months to live.

"Doc, what am I gonna do?"

Now this old doc has been around a while, and he says, "What I recommend to you is this: Marry a Basco lady and move to Mountain City."

"What good will that do?"

"Not a thing," the doc says. "But it'll make them six months seem like an eternity."

On glass shelves in a long glass case near Tremewan's front counter, beaded Indian jewelry is neatly displayed. Necklaces and earrings and bracelets and hairpins. Change purses and shoulder bags and moccasins for babies, children, and adults. On the wall behind the case hang several cradle boards—tanned buckskin stretched over light, sturdy frames with laced, built-in pockets to carry infants. All of these have been made by Indians on the Duck Valley Reservation. Lou pays the artist for each piece up front, and then sells them for the same price she paid for them. On a tag connected to each piece is the price, the artist's name, and sometimes a phone number. Among and between them, open boxes contain strings of beads of several different colors.

For the most part, the people who buy these items are other Indians from Duck Valley, or Indians coming to Owyhee from another reservation for a powwow or a rodeo. Tremewan's Store is not a "trading post." There are no miniature totem poles or buffalo coin banks for sale. No dream catchers. No lithographic postcards of stoic elders. There's no profoundly sad wooden chief on the front porch smoking a cigar. Voyne is usually on the front porch, and he won't smoke anything.

I told Mel that in colleges all over the country you're not supposed to say "Indian." You're supposed to say "Native American."

"These Indians call themselves Indians," Mel said. "If they start calling themselves Native Americans, I'll call them that."

Mel was teaching me some Paiute expressions.

"How do you say hello?" I asked.

"You just said it."

"What do you mean?"

"Repeat what you just said."

"How do you say hello in Paiute?"

"There it is again."

"What are you talking about?"

"Not *what*," he said. *"How."*

He raised his flat palm up in the air beside his ear.

"Very funny," I said.

"That's the Indian version of 'Who's on first?' I could've run it out a bit longer, but I let you off easy. That's an old one. They probably come up with that many, many moons ago."

In 1869, on a flat rise above Mountain City, the U.S. Army built Fort McGinnis to protect the settlers from the Indians, and from the beginning, the structure puzzled the local citizenry.

The fort had a few problems. Its first problem was its size. The tiny wooden fort could fit perhaps thirty people, but only if they stood shoulder to shoulder, packed together and slightly contorted in the fashion of future record-breaking attempts involving phone booths or Volkswagen Bugs. Its second problem was water. The fort was a half mile from the river, and for a simple geologic reason (solid rock), the fort lacked a well. Had the Indians ever laid siege, the fort's cramped inhabitants would have been the ones performing the rain dance, their necks craned, their mouths upturned and open like baby birds. The last problem was more subtle, more difficult for the army of the new West to comprehend, and it was this: the bands of Shoshone who lived in the area were a peaceful people.

Except for ceremonial purposes, displays of might and military artistry, the fort was never used. After a number of vacant years, the practical citizens of Mountain City tore it down and used the wood to build entrances to the mines. Except for old photographs, no trace of the stronghold remains. On that flat rise a small electrical power station now stands, formidable. A barbed-wire fence surrounds it to keep out cows.

On the western boundary of the old Tremewan Ranch, a creek runs through a meadow in the shadow of the Independence Range. The creek is called Stump Creek, after a particular tree stump which took Gramps and his brother and their dad and a team of horses two full days to uproot. Gramps says it was that stump, not his father or brother or any person, which taught him the meaning of the word *stubborn*. He was a boy then and had just begun to learn how a thing can persist against a seemingly irrevocable will for it to die.

Beside the creek was an old log cabin which some prospector had built and abandoned and which the Tremewans fixed up and stayed in when they were building fence, or haying, or clearing the meadow.

Though they lost the ranch in 1930, Gramps continued to use the cabin for nearly thirty years as a base camp for hunting and fishing trips, for picnics with family. No road led to the cabin. Few people then (or now) knew of the place, and so for

Gramps and Grandma and my mother and her sisters, it was a place they had to themselves. Fed by snowmelt, the creek, as it passes the cabin, was cold and clear and about a foot deep, and there, in the foothills, it ran year-round. A stand of quakies lined the creek, and Gramps encircled the cabin with a fence of dead-fall to keep out the sheep that passed by on their way to their summer range up in the mountains.

The cabin is in ruins now, its foundation logs sunken and swallowed by earth, the roof gone, unaccounted, the frame vacant and open to the clouds. Grass and thistle grow through the floorboards. Nailed here and there to the exterior log walls are tomato can lids of various diameters, thirty or forty of them. Toward the end, before Gramps finally gave up the cabin for good, he'd used the lids as Band-Aids for a woodpecker problem.

When Gramps was a boy, he invented a mousetrap for the cabin. He took a roof shingle and through its middle put a staple, which functioned as a hinge, so the shingle would flex. Then he filled a bucket with water and fixed the staple to the edge of it. Half the shingle served as a ramp for the mice to run up, and the other half was like a diving board over the water, with a piece of bacon rind tacked on the end to draw them out. For the mice, it was like walking the plank. They headed out on the shingle unsuspecting, and their own weight did them in. They slid down into the drink, which was deep enough so they couldn't jump out, and they drowned. And it was fully automatic. Reloaded itself. One night between supper and bedtime, Gramps caught seventeen mice in that bucket.

Mice are a problem in Mountain City. At my grandparents' place, they run between the apartment walls and up above the ceiling tiles. Some nights at dinner, when the mice start scampering above us, Mel says, "And . . . they're off!"

Grandma knows there's a mice problem, but she doesn't know anything about racetracks. She doesn't know the mice are in the ceiling. She can't hear them, thank God. Gramps can hear them, but he doesn't say anything to Grandma. He figures what she doesn't know won't hurt her.

Over the years, Gramps has upgraded from the bucket model he used as a boy, and now he uses d-Con and spring-loaded mousetraps. He places them strategically in high-traffic areas. The laundry room. The cabinet under the sink. In the spring, he usually finds two or three limp victims each morning.

Tremewan's Store has its own mice troubles, but Mel looks upon the matter philosophically:

"Animals have all the time in the world. *That's* why they're so mischievous. They don't have anybody telling them to get something done by noon, or to be someplace and not be late. They can just work at a problem until they get her done. Take the mice we get in the store here. The Macaroni Bandits. They know we got the place sealed up pretty good, but that don't worry them. If it takes them all day to get through the floor and into the macaroni, that's just fine. They're not punching the clock. Take the cows out in the meadow. They only hustle around when Jim's out there hollering at them to get a move on, and his dog's nipping at their heels. Mice, on the other hand, having never been domesticated, don't have that anxiety. They don't stand around worrying about mousetraps and all the things they got to get done before their number gets called. That's an advantage.

"Animals excel at relaxation. Sure they work at surviving. But when that's squared away, they let up some. Not us. We always have to be doing something. Producing. Time's money. I've got it figured out. I've been studying this. I know it doesn't look like it, but I have. Pretty soon I won't be wearing this green apron every day. Stick around and watch. Pretty soon this Basco's gonna start exercising his animal nature."

Mel isn't joking about retirement. He'd retire yesterday if he had his way. He's been working at the store for almost forty years, ten hours a day, six days a week, and for the first fifteen years, it was seven days a week. He's tired, worn-out, and he complains in indirect ways all the time, especially in the evenings when the Black Velvet has kicked in.

"How was *your* day, honey?" Mel asks Lou at dinner. Lou ignores him. She knows this routine.

"Oh, that's right. *Your* day was just like mine. The green apron drill. Pork and beans and customers. That's right. I forgot. You and Mitch and me, and Greg there, we all spent the day at the store. Of course, *Greg* did take his mountain bike for a spin in the middle of the afternoon. How did that go, son?"

Mel often calls me son. He even introduces me to people as his son. Sometimes I correct him, sometimes I don't. "It's good exercise," I say. "You should try it. Gets you off your feet for a while. See the country."

I'm the only one at the store who takes time off each day to ride a bike, or play cards with Eddie, or to go up and visit with Grandma or with Rosella. I've suggested we all should do that, take a few hours off each day while the other three cover the store, but no one wants to try it.

"I *should* try that, you're right," Mel says. "As soon as I retire, I'll take up mountain biking. That and a few other things. I'm going to get some hobbies. Right now I don't have any hobbies besides the Black Velvet. Lou's got plenty of hobbies, and as soon as I hang that apron up, I'm taking after her. She's worried that if we retire I'll take on the Black Velvet full-time, and I won't leave some slack for other hobbies. Isn't that right, Lou?"

Lou doesn't answer. She refuses to encourage him in any way. Lou doesn't want to retire. She's worked at the store just as long as Mel, but she looks forward to each day. She isn't as extroverted as Mel, and, on the surface, he seems more enthusiastic. But much of that is acting, role playing. Mel knows that customers expect him to make them laugh, to cheer them up, and so many days Mel feels like a magician who's tired of pulling the same rabbit out of the same hat. He's tired of being onstage. There's a sourness beneath his store persona that he suppresses until the Black Velvet conjures it out of him each night. Lou is quieter, and she doesn't perform. She enjoys the customers and the several women who come in each day to visit with her. These conversations aren't on public display, and they run deeper than most of Mel's conversations. They satisfy and engage her, and when they are done, she returns to the tasks and routines of the store. She also has a full life outside of the store—the Quilting Society, the Home-makers Club, the School Board, hunting trips each fall, her grandchildren's activities in Elko. She doesn't just go home after dinner and fall asleep on the couch. She reads each night— Nevada history, Western history, *National Geographic,* the day's newspaper from Reno.

My cousin Mitch has worked in the store full-time since he was twenty, and he's forty now. Mel and Lou always figured he'd marry, and then he and his wife would continue running the store when they retired. But Mitch hasn't married, and he feels about the same way Mel does. He's ready to do something else. He's not sure what, but he's ready for it.

Mel and Lou's other two children help out in the store often, but they both have their own families and careers. Dan works for the mines, and he and his family live in Elko. Molly lives on a ranch that she and her husband manage for an absentee California millionaire, and she works part-time in Elko as a dental hygienist. Neither of them wants to take over the store.

There are no young couples, no young families, in Mountain City who could take over the store, because there are no young couples and no young families in Mountain City. There's no one in their thirties. Mitch, at forty, is his decade's only representative. Graham and I are the only ones in our twenties, and we come and go. There's no one to wait for either, no heirs, no successors. There are no children in Mountain City. No teenagers, no toddlers. A few kids live out on area ranches, but they have legacies of their own.

People around here are pretty used to the store's idiosyncratic credit policy, and it would be hard to convince an outside buyer to perpetuate a system built completely on trust. That sort of thing takes familiarity and time, a sense of shared history. But first, before any of that, there has to be a buyer to convince, and

Mel and Lou and Mitch aren't too confident they could ever find one to come out to the sagebrush and have a go at it.

Mel talks about one day donating all the store's inventory to charity. A big truck from Boise would come, and they'd spend a few days running dollies loaded with boxes out the back warehouse door. Then, eventually, the store would be empty. The aisles of shelves empty, the warehouse shelves empty, the coolers empty, the deep freeze empty, the soda case empty, the dairy case empty, the produce bins empty, the meat counter empty, the registers empty. All that would remain would be Mel's Basco jokes hanging alone from the walls and the ceiling. BASCO DONUT SEEDS. Then Mel would take the ring of keys from his pocket and walk around the outside of the store. He'd stop at each door and lock it, ceremoniously, listening for each dead bolt to click flush in its hole. Then he'd walk away. Call it good.

Lou can see the end coming. She can't run the store by herself, and in a few years, maybe less, Mel and Mitch won't be showing up for work anymore. I sometimes imagine myself coming back to Mountain City when I'm old, bringing with me children and grandchildren, and pointing to the foundations of a building off the highway and saying, "There, that's what I've been telling you about all this time. That's where the store used to be. And there, look over there . . ."

It's two minutes after five, and Mel is in the kitchen of the store fixing his first highball.

"I didn't hear your alarm go off," I say. Mel has the new travel alarm he ordered from Black Velvet sitting on top of the butcher case.

"I don't think I'm gonna need it. Just before it was set to go off, I started getting the shakes and tics, and somehow I knew it was time." Mel is histrionic, his face twitching, his hands and arms wild.

"A Jekyll and Hyde thing," I say.

"That's right. But I got the antidote."

"Don't you mean the poison?"

"You think so?"

"You know what I think."

"You and everybody else. But the way I see it is that if I were to wake up in the morning and start hitting the Black Velvet first thing, *then* I'd start worrying. But I don't do that. It doesn't affect what goes on here at the store. I know that some people probably think I'm an alcoholic, but not to me I'm not. And you know what?"

"What?"

"I'm happy. And you know what else? I stop sometimes. I do. Like before a doctor checkup. I'll stop for a few days."

"And are you irritable?"

"Hell yes. Like a grizzly bear just come out of hibernation. Hungry as hell, but not for food."

"Then you start up again, and you feel fine."

"Just like that. And I don't worry about it. Son, I got hamburger to grind."

Mel takes his highball out to the butcher's counter, leaving me standing there in the kitchen. At Tremewan's Store, if you want to get out of a conversation, there's always something urgent to attend to that isn't urgent until you decide it is.

A quarter to six and Mel's having another highball. Larry Oth-eim has joined him.

"My nephew here's been telling me all my faults. Going right down the list. Where I could stand some improvements. He's got it all figured out. I'm sixty. He's half that and some change. I'm not saying he's wrong. Am I saying that? No."

Six o'clock. Larry's bought his groceries and gone home.

"I'll tell you what, son. I *have* given it up. Six weeks. Two months. And does it *change* anything? Do we talk in the evenings? I ask questions, questions about feelings, and she just looks at me, looks at me like, 'Shouldn't you know the answer to that?' But I don't. I don't know.

"It's different when we're not in the store. Like Labor Day. We just took off for a drive in the country. We still don't talk much, but it's different, the atmosphere's different, it changes. And we're easy with each other. But after we put a day in at the store, what are we supposed to say to each other?

"And after dinner I don't get to go home, take my shoes off, and sit on my couch like most guys. We go to Grandma and Gramps's, which is fine, it really is, fine. I ask Gramps about what happened today in the world, and that's good for him. But it's not my home. I've been eating dinner at my in-laws' house every night for thirty-five years. No, since I was sixteen, forty-four years, can you imagine?"

Six-fifteen. We're getting ready to close, go home for dinner. Lou's putting the day's credit slips in alphabetical order. I'm turning off the lights to all the coolers. Mel's cleaning up around the meat counter.

"God, Melvin, did you give Curtis Harney credit again?" Lou says loudly, exasperated. She's holding up the credit slip, staring at it.

Mel walks up to the front. The muscles in his face are flaccid, and the skin sags heavily, like a face in a cartoon.

"Mel, he's owed us for six months. He hasn't got a job, and he isn't about to get one."

"I know it," Mel says, resigned. "I shouldn't have done it. But there were lots of people around. Normally I say no."

Mel is looking down, like a kid prepared for a reprimand, but Lou seems satisfied with his answer. She's been in the same situation many times, and she understands. If she's upset with him, it's not about the credit policy. There is no credit policy at Tremewan's Store, and never has been. There's always tension swirling around its discussion, which takes the form of a power struggle. Mel and Lou and Mitch are equal partners in the family business. There's no hierarchy among them, each has a different breaking point, and there are no store meetings to update one another on when these breaking points have been reached. It's not uncommon for a delinquent customer to ask Mel for credit and get rejected, then wait until Mel goes to the back and ask Lou or Mitch and get a third or fourth chance.

"I know this might be against tradition," I say, "but maybe there should be a list. Like an eighty-six list at a bar. We could put it back in the kitchen."

"You're full of suggestions today, aren't you, son?" Mel says, turning to me. His tone is belligerent. I've never heard this tone from him in my life.

"Credit isn't any of your business, you know that, son? You don't run this store. You're family, and you're here to help, but you come and go, and this isn't any of your business."

"Mel, stop it," Lou says. "That's enough. He can say whatever he wants."

"No, no, I don't think so. He thinks he has all the ideas, but not this time. I've heard just about enough from him. He needs to know that."

Mel turns and walks to the back, gets his coat, and leaves out the back door.

"I'm sorry about what I said last night," Mel says.

I've just walked in the front door of the store with Gramps. It's a few minutes before opening. Gramps stands off to the side and doesn't say anything while Mel gives me a hug. Mel didn't go to Grandma and Gramps's for dinner the night before.

"You forgive me, don't you?"

"I do."

"I love you, son. I'm sorry. We both know why that happened, don't we?"

I nod my head.

"It gets away from me sometimes. It does. Gramps and I used to have a highball together sometimes at the end of the day."

Mel looks over at Gramps. Gramps looks up but doesn't say anything.

"That's been years. Gramps has to look after his health. I'll bet you don't have a highball but twice a year."

"Three times, I'd say," Gramps says.

"Three times, that's right. I forgot about that other one. But pretty much now I'm on my own, and sometimes I take it too far and I'm sorry."

"That's okay," I say.

"I've got a lazy mind," Mel says. "Not much willpower. I don't know what to do with myself. That worries me. Don't like reading. Never have. If there's a show on the TV worth watching, I'll watch it. But I'm tired. I am tired. I'll tell you what I *would* like to know more about and that's pigeons. If I had more time, I'd study pigeons. We've got this guy, comes here every year in the spring, right here to Mountain City, and he's got a truck loaded up with cages and cages of pigeons, hundreds of them. Then exactly at noon on one particular day, he pulls a wire that's connected to every one of them cages, and then all those doors swing wide, and *bang,* it's like a cloud of wings flapping into the sky. Sacramento, California, that's where he's from, and that's where those pigeons are headed. Something about the exact distance between Sacramento and Mountain City makes this the ideal place. And every year those pigeons make it home, and he times them, studies the numbers. He's some kind of scientist. Now if you took *me* to Sacramento, California, and let *me* loose on one of them busy streets, I don't think I'd have the faintest notion what to do. Not without help, not without a map. If I had to just reckon from my insides, it'd be a crapshoot. I'd start walking, I guess, but I just as soon might strike the Pacific as Mountain City. I'd need help. I know where home is and I don't. But those pigeons know it both ways, and the second way is a mystery. Now *that* is something I'd like to know more about, is pigeons."

Tribal law prohibits the sale of liquor on the Duck Valley Reservation. The closest place to buy alcohol is in Mountain City, at Tremewan's Store.

Because the canyon between Mountain City and Owyhee is so winding and narrow, the maximum speed limit in several places is twenty-five miles per hour. There's a particular turn on that stretch of road we call Drunk Indians' Turn, for all the Indians fished out of the river there where they drove over the edge and into the Owyhee.

The Thompson family lives on a ranch in a small valley on the south side of the Trail Creek Road, a few miles outside of Mountain City. For years, an Indian named Pete Whiterock helped them with all the tasks of the ranch. Pete and his young boy Woody lived in the bunkhouse behind the ranch house. Who Woody's mother was or where she was, then or later, I don't know. Pete was quiet and hardworking and reliable, and one day he left Woody and the ranch and didn't come back. Woody was seven years old.

Woody still had relatives on the reservation who would have taken him in, but the boy didn't want to leave the ranch. So Norman and Ellen took Woody to raise. Woody played each day with Margie, the Thompsons' daughter, who was his age, and he looked up to John, who was five or six years older.

There was then and is still now only one school within eighty miles of Mountain City, a government school on the reservation. Growing up, my cousins took the bus there each morning from Mountain City. On the bus already were John and Margie and Woody, coming down from Trail Creek. They all played together after school in town and spent weekends together out on the Thompson Ranch.

After Woody's father left, the Indian children from the reservation teased Woody mercilessly for choosing to live with the Thompsons. They called him Whitey Whiterock and not Woody. They called him Apple. Red on the outside and white on the inside.

I knew Woody later, when he was about fifteen. I was five or six, and he seemed to me then more like a man than any boy I'd ever known: dark, brooding, quiet, as if there had never been a boy to grow up from. He was neither friendly nor mean, just distant. He kept mostly to himself. I would see Woody when we went out to the Thompsons' for some event, a picnic or branding, and when I would say hello, he would nod, saying nothing, and his face would be empty, expressionless, and then I would feel empty and wonder what I'd done wrong.

Tremewan's Store has been broken into many times since Gramps bought it forty years ago. Each time the thieves have been caught, they've been Indians from the reservation. No money has ever been taken. The money is kept in a safe in the back. After closing, the drawers to the cash registers are left open and empty and in plain sight through the front windows. Alcohol has been stolen. The back door has been kicked in. The front window smashed. In a series of thefts which spread out over weeks, cases of liquor were stolen, with no sign of forced entry. Mel finally discovered that the thieves must be lowering themselves down from a vent in the roof. Gramps, Mel, and Colon Perry, the deputy sheriff, waited inside the store with rifles each night for a week. When the thieves came again, they were caught. Three Indian teenagers, two from the reservation, and Woody.

Norman and Ellen had been having a difficult time with Woody for a year or more before the robberies. He'd stolen the car several times and had been arrested for drunk driving.

As justice of the peace, Gramps would have heard the case, had it not been his family's store that had been robbed. The two boys from the reservation were younger than Woody and received probation and community service. Woody was to be sent to a juvenile lockdown in Elko.

The day after the sentencing Woody blew his brains out with Norman's rifle.

The highway cutting through the heart of the Duck Valley Reservation borders open range, and in winter, at dusk, cattle and wild horses linger on the sun-soaked tar. On the western horizon, the colors of sunset deepen and fade. If you're smart, you'll pay attention to signs, keep your eyes on the road. You've got no one to blame but yourself.

Stanley Griswold wakes before dawn. He rises from bed and dresses himself, his fingers deftly capturing each shirt button, snapping them into place. He pulls on his boots and walks out into the lobby of the Clifton Hotel, an old Basque hotel which for years has been a boardinghouse for elderly cowboys and sheepmen. This is his home. He isn't Basque, but that doesn't matter. There used to be more Basques before, but none of the Basque hotels was ever exclusive. Stanley's lived in the hotel for thirty years. He used to take a room on the second floor, but there's no elevator in the hotel, and he can no longer climb stairs. Stanley is ninety-six.

It's April and the snow is still thick on top of the Rubies, the mountain range running south out of Elko down toward Ely. At 6 a.m., the lobby door opens and Stanley comes out to the pickup idling in front of the hotel. He is tall and thin, all legs and arms and neck, like he was made from elastic and not bone. I slide over on the bench beside George, Stanley gets in, slowly, and we drive to breakfast.

Each morning my uncle George picks up Stanley and they go first to breakfast and then to their rawhide shop. They sit in the same booth at the same Basque restaurant, the Toki Ona. This morning is Easter morning and I'm joining them. It was either rawhide or mass. If I'd still been at my aunt Sarah's when Grandma woke up, it would have been mass.

We've just sat down when Louie Arano, an old Basco, comes in the door. Louie takes Stanley to dinner each night, and comes to breakfast three or four mornings a week.

"Hemen gaude etorri garelako!" he says, grinning, his arms wide, and then he joins us in the booth. What Louie has said translates to: "We're here, because we came!" Typical Basco humor. Louie is short and squat with long white hair and a white beard, an imp. Neither George nor Stanley acknowledges him. Not even a nod. It's as if, after having spent so much time together, there's no need to mark the comings and goings.

The waitress brings coffee. "I see you've got another eligible bachelor in the group," she says to Louie and nods over at me. "Aren't you worried about the competition?"

"No ma'am," Louie answers, confidently. "Stanley and I are in another league altogether. Women can feel the experience in us tugging like a magnet at their belt buckles."

"Is that right?" she says.

"That's right."

Louie winks at me. I remind myself that Nevada's a place where plenty of women wear belt buckles. Stanley's looking straight ahead, and I can't read his face at all. Maybe he's lost in memories, maybe a belt-buckled girl he made it with in his prime, seventy-five years ago.

The food arrives. Eggs, bacon, and toast. George and Stanley are smoking. Stanley's smoking a cigar. I'm wondering if everything I've heard about health is some kind of conspiracy.

Louie leans across the table. "These old-timers, you know, won't listen to reason. Stanley knows that cigar's gonna kill him someday."

"The sooner the better."

It's the first thing Stanley's said all morning. I think he's joking, but it's hard to tell.

The rawhide shop isn't much of a shop. It's the small back room of the house George lived in before marrying my aunt Sarah. They've been married a few years, both having been previously divorced. George had been a cowboy all his life, and as a younger man had been much closer to his horse than to any woman.

I don't think the shop has ever been cleaned. Thin strips of rawhide lie scattered about the trampled carpet. Cobwebs adorn the four ceiling corners. The window glass is stained yellow, opaque from years of smoke. The room has three chairs, one each for George, Stanley, and Louie. Louie's gone to mass and I'm sitting in his chair. A workbench leans against the far wall from the door, piled over with cutting tools. From the near wall hang several sets of reins, some new, some old but newly repaired. A bucket of water holds the room's center.

Rawhide reins from this shop are known in small circles all

over the state. George and Stanley and Louie don't advertise, they don't have a company logo or name, but they can't keep up with demand. They figure people will wait, and they do.

There are only three or four other shops in the Northwest that still braid rawhide by hand. It takes time. The rawhide has to be first soaked for days in lye, in the bathtub in the next room. Then it's soaked in vinegar and water to cancel the lye. It then takes the three of them over thirty hours of working together, at a pace which could only generously be termed moderate, usually a full week of mornings (they all nap in the afternoons), to finish one set of reins.

George and Stanley set to work as soon as we arrive. George braids the strips of rawhide through a half-finished set of reins, a process he learned from his father and from Stanley, who was his father's friend. Stanley soaks the hardened, recently cut strips in the bucket, placing the tips in a groove in a block of wood that floats atop the water. The tips stay dry this way, keeping their points, while the trailings are submerged, softening. While Stanley waits on the soaking strips, he rubs a soap-and-oil compound into a newly finished set of reins. This will keep the reins malleable so that they won't harden or dry out over time.

Spring mornings in northern Nevada are beautiful, the air clean and cool, the light soft, but you wouldn't know it from inside the shop. George has turned the heater on and the two are smoking again, Stanley chewing on another cigar.

As I watch them work, asking questions, the room slowly fills with smoke. My eyes begin to water. I cough a little here and there. The two go on working. Soon, all I can smell is electric heat and smoke, and I'm not sure if the whole place isn't on fire. I cough some more and George notices.

"Sorry about that. Sometimes it gets to where we can't see from here to the door or make each other out through the fog."

George cracks the window about a half inch.

After an hour or so, Louie shows up.

"Kind of like one of them Indian sweat lodges in here," he says to me. "Except nobody in here's praying to nothing. I spend half my time in church praying for these two. I keep telling them there's no horses in hell, but they won't listen."

The three of them work at the rawhide, all the while Louie making conversation, George making a short comment here and there, Stanley quiet.

"Stanley here was a batch supervisor with your great-grandfather, you know," George says.

"What's a batch supervisor do?" I ask.

Stanley looks up from the strings he's holding. "Certain parasites infect the cattle's hide. Scabies, they call it. Back then you had to dip them all in a vat to cure it. Hell of a task getting a cow to take a swim in a ditch full of solution. Charlie Tremewan and I used to oversee the process for the county."

"And he couldn't stand watermelon," Louie adds, laughing.

"It's a wonder he didn't shoot you dead, Louie," says George.

And then, without any special remark or notice, the three of them start talking about my great-grandfather. Not one of them is related to me by blood, and not one knows they are telling me more about Gramps's dad than I've ever heard before without asking first. With Gramps, if I want to know something historical, I had better ask. The distant past for me isn't distant for him. The losses still ache. You can tell by the way he pauses while telling a story that he doesn't want to dig further into the memory. The people he describes, though dead, are still people. They will never become characters.

"*Watermelon* was *not* that man's favorite fruit," Louie says. "That's for sure. Charlie and I worked together awhile for the Western Pacific. He and Oliver and I all worked as brakemen then. It was after they lost the ranch. That job was hard work and a lot of walking, time on your feet, and Charlie, like a lot of them old-timers, like Stanley here, would as soon ride a horse a hundred miles as walk one. Well, a man would look forward to sitting down once during the day to enjoy his lunch. Charlie hated watermelon. And I was just a kid, you know, so I got it in my head one morning to sneak a watermelon rind in his lunch pail. You should have seen him open it up at noon. I've never seen a man's face turn so sour in my life. Couldn't touch his lunch."

Louie's smile seems as wide as the room, and he's shaking his head, playing the scene over in his memory.

"Now, *who knows* how a crazy thing like that got to be common knowledge, but it did. Guys on his crew used to wrap watermelon in packages and give them to him for Christmas. And he never was good-natured about it, like he was about near everything else. Which is why I suppose the practice kept up.

"Back then, you know, it used to be that the young guys would look after the older ones, take the tougher jobs, the more physical work, leave the older ones some slack, keep them on the payroll. It's not like that anymore. Progress, you know. Efficiency."

The shop goes quiet with hands working at rawhide. I have a sense that these three must now be thinking of something I'll never know in the context just described. But I am keenly aware that its essence has been demonstrated all morning. George and Louie looking after Stanley. Breakfast every morning. The rawhide. It has been demonstrated by men who do not neatly fit the stereotype of the Western man. The primitive. The stoic. It's no wonder that Stanley has lived to ninety-six, still holding reins each day though he can no longer ride, still speaking the language of his life with men who know what it means to him, still useful, still making something of value.

In the summertime, Louie Arano mows about twenty lawns a week. When he's not mowing lawns, he's spending time with Stanley or George or driving some old Basco he knows to the doctor's office. Louie is seventy-two.

After my great-aunt, Lenore Zabala, Grandma's youngest sister, was diagnosed with cancer, Louie mowed her lawn every week for three summers. He sometimes left groceries on her porch. At first, Lenore tried to pay him, but he wouldn't let her. Louie won't take money from anyone. Later, Lenore started leaving a fifth of whiskey on the corner of the side porch, near where Louie parked his pickup. She thought he might make an exception to his philanthropic policy. She was right.

Lenore used to cuss Louie out as he put the lawn mower back in the bed of his pickup and got ready to leave. Lenore could make a sailor blush. She used the C word freely. You can see what Louie was up against. "Okay, *atso zikina,*" Louie would say. "You win." Lenore didn't mind that Louie called her a dirty old woman. What she minded was him leaving. She was dying, and she wanted some company. "Sit your ass down and talk to me." So Louie would sit on Lenore's side porch, take a sip of whiskey, and they'd talk for a while before he was off to mow someone else's lawn.

The morning of Lenore's funeral, Louie didn't go out to the cemetery for the burial. A reception was being held later that day at Lenore's house, and so after the mass Louie went home, put his lawn mower in his pickup, and went over there and mowed the lawn.

If you could have seen him on that summer morning in Elko, Nevada, you would know everything I want you to know about Louie. You would have seen a short, old Basco pushing a lawn mower across a yard beneath a modest oak tree in front of a small, one-story house. You would have noticed immediately his straight, clean, shoulder-length, white hair, his finely trimmed white beard, his pressed gray suit and oiled leather shoes and thin black bolo tie. All around you would have been the smell of clippings and gasoline and morning, and you would have seen him as he turned at the end of a row, and you would have watched as his slow, measured steps moved forward across the yard.

Summer mornings in Mountain City are cold and brisk, but as the day unfolds, the air warms and settles evenly. The brutal winter winds are gone, and the anxiety among us has gone with them. Then, my grandparents are healthy and spry and rarely inside the house. Each morning at exactly ten before eight, Gramps finishes his breakfast, takes his cap from the top of the refrigerator, puts it on, and gets his green sweatshirt from its hook on the back of the hall closet door. He comes back to the kitchen and kisses Grandma on the cheek as she watches *Good Morning America*. She's doing her quilting or writing a letter, and she smiles and tells him to have a good day. Then Gramps leaves the house and walks down to the store. In winter, Gramps does exactly these same things, this same ritual, but the silence that attends those mornings is as different as the contrary seasons. It is as cold as the wind.

In late morning, when the chill is broken, Grandma tends her small garden between the house and the garage. She kneels down, lowering her short, blocked figure slowly, and through her polyester pants her two mechanical knees press rounded cups in the soil. She wears a green apron from Tremewan's Store, using its two deep pockets for her scissors, trowel, and gloves. There, along the side of the house, purple pansies bloom in one long row. Grandma planted them in spring, just after the frost. The growing season in Mountain City is short, eighty days frost to frost, and so there are many flowers, like white tulips or bright red geraniums, that Grandma wants to plant but can't because they'd winter-kill.

In the afternoon, Grandma reads romances in her lawn chair beneath an aspen tree at the edge of the yard. From there, she can look down on the river and the meadow and the hills. Sometimes she falls asleep with the book open in her lap and her chin resting on her chest, or she reads until dusk comes and she can barely make out the letters on the page.

When Gramps isn't down at the store, he works outside, clipping and raking the yard, or trimming back the thin new shoots and dead branches of the golden willows that surround the apartment building. Gramps is the only person in town who won't mow his lawn with a motor-driven lawn mower. He doesn't like the noise. And he won't let me or Mitch or Mel mow the lawn for him with Mel's lawn mower, which has a bag to catch the clippings. Taking care of his yard is something Gramps can still do, and as the number of such things diminishes, it's not something he'll let others do for him.

Each night after dinner, in the long, dim blue light of dusk, Grandma and Gramps go for a walk together. They walk along the shoulder of the highway past Mel and Lou's, past the Forest

Service and the store. In the grass along the road, fireweed blooms, tall and purple, and magpies settle onto fence posts and light poles. Jackrabbits scurry in and out of the cover of the grass, and the river, coursing along its banks, can be heard in the distance. Grandma and Gramps turn left onto a dirt road leading down to a flat wooden bridge that spans the Owyhee. The bridge is narrow and without guardrails, and below it, on its west side, the river bends and juts into the meadow. There, the river runs deep and slows and so is safe to swim in while the main current rushes on. I used to swim there in the summers with my cousins, and Gramps remembers swimming there once when he was a boy, the time his family came to Mountain City from their ranch for the Fourth of July. He remembers a bridge there, in the same spot, though it was not the same bridge; he remembers the swimming hole, and he remembers the cold of the current beneath the water's surface.

My grandparents stand on the bridge and look down into the river or out over the meadows and the hills. I don't know what they say to each other then. My guess is that they say little, but I have seen them holding hands as they walk back home, retracing their steps up the dirt road and the highway. What I feel then is a strange mixture of relief and gladness and melancholy. The winter is gone and it is summer. But fall in northern Nevada is short and fleeting, and I don't know what will become of us all when winter comes again.

The last time Stanley and George and Louie had breakfast at the Toki Ona, Stanley forgot to leave the tip. That's his job, leaving the tip. Two dollars. So the waitress comes up to him as they're leaving and says, "Wasn't I good enough today, Stanley? Not even a buck?" That caught Stanley off guard, and it took him a minute before he started rummaging around for his billfold. Now he won't go back. He won't tolerate rude behavior. They'd been eating breakfast there every morning for four years, with the same waitress. Before that, they'd been over at the Star Hotel, until something happened that Stanley wouldn't stand for. Louie says that, in the last twenty years, Stanley has eighty-sixed every restaurant in town at least once. He says they had a record going at the Toki Ona, a real streak. They're on their second go-round now at the Commercial Hotel, where nobody local goes to eat because the food's so lousy.

Stanley has quit smoking. Ninety-six years old. He'd smoked since he was a teenager. Decided to quit. Cigars. Cigarettes. Quit. Cold turkey, whatever that means. Louie says that Stanley had been reading up on tobacco, and the evidence was pretty convincing, hard to ignore. It's been three months now, and George, who still smokes a pack a day, feels alone, isolated, a bit ostracized. At the rawhide shop, Stanley has asked him to crack the window quite a bit more than usual. Let in the fresh air.

I was telling Gramps about Stanley, about how, when the weather's nice, George parks the truck as far as he thinks he can get away with from whatever door he and Stanley are walking to. I told Gramps how Stanley can still read the newspaper without glasses.

"Not everybody's so lucky, are they, Gramps?"

"Is he lucky?"

"What do you think?"

"I'm not talking about his eyes."

A Shoshone man named Evan comes into the store a few times a month. Mel calls him Old Snickerpuss. He's probably seventy years old. He walks slowly, with a cane, and he wears hearing aids in both ears. He's almost always scowling. He shows up well after five, just before closing, when Mel has already dived deep into his pool of Black Velvet. The old Indian comes back to the meat counter and orders a couple pounds of baloney. He barks the order. "Baloney! Two!"

"Keep an eye on Old Snickerpuss," Mel says to me, and then he adds, after noting my surprise, "Don't worry. He can't hear a thing. Those hearing aids might as well be wax. Snickerpuss here loves sweets, and he's been stealing Snickers bars from me for years. Puts them right in his jacket pocket. Eats them on the front porch while he waits for his wife. What the Old Snicker-bandit doesn't know is that I've jacked up the price of baloney on him. He's been buying gourmet baloney for a long time."

Mel turns and hands Evan the baloney he's sliced and wrapped and priced while talking to me, and Mel says, "There you go, Evan. Baloney."

Evan takes the package and says gruffly, "Okay," and he walks up to the front register, which is beside the candy bar rack.

Mel finishes his glass, pours another highball, and says, "Old Snickerpuss is crooked as a dog's hind leg, but this Basco can play that game, too."

The phone rings at Tremewan's Store, and Lou answers it. It's my great-aunt Ruth, Gramps's sister, and she wants to speak with Gramps. Lou hands him the phone and returns to her register. It's late in the morning on Saturday, and the store is busy, full of customers. Autumn has descended on Mountain City and so have the deer hunters. Three men in orange and camouflage stand waiting at one front counter while Mel sells them licenses. At the other counter, four people wait in line with their shopping carts full of groceries—business as usual for a Saturday morning. An hour passes, and in that time, several more hunters come in. Mel and Lou make a few suggestions. Lou is the best shot in our family. The mountain goat on the wall around the corner from the dairy case is hers. Beneath it is a large bulletin board pinned with hunting pictures and newspaper clippings— all of and about our family and people around Mountain City. Next to the bulletin board are several U.S. Geological Survey topographical maps of the area. Mel calls this area of the store the War Room.

Customers come and go, and during a brief break in the

activity, Lou asks Gramps, who has been standing silently beside the phone the whole time, "What did Aunt Ruth say?"

"She said that Syd died this morning."

These words hang in the air. Gramps's face is a mask, utterly without inflection. His brother, Syd, had been in the hospital off and on for a year, battling cancer. "She says there isn't going to be a funeral. Syd didn't want one."

The previous spring, Grandma and Gramps had visited Syd at his home in Boise. They had planned on staying a few days with him, but ended up checking into a motel the first night and driving back to Mountain City the next morning. Syd had been drunk in the middle of the afternoon. He'd been rude and mean-spirited, and Gramps wouldn't put up with him. This kind of behavior had been characteristic of Syd ever since his wife died, three years earlier. He had not been that way before. That visit to Boise was the last time Gramps had seen him.

We each tell Gramps that we're sorry, but no one moves to hug Gramps except for Mel, who is not a Tremewan and is not limited by the same stoic blood that constricts Lou, Mitch, and me. Gramps receives Mel stiffly, his arms at his sides. Mel doesn't care. He hugs him anyway, too long, so long that it's painful to watch, as if Mel's taking up the time the rest of us won't take.

Lou gets on the phone and calls Grandma up at the house, tells her what's happened. Gramps interrupts. "Tell her there isn't going to be a funeral. Tell her he didn't want one." Lou passes this on and then says, "Grandma says she's coming down."

Grandma isn't in the store for three seconds before she starts raging, her eyes wild, her teeth bared like badger's. "It's not fair!"

she says furiously, lending each word equal weight. She takes Gramps's hands in both of hers and squeezes them tightly. She's right beneath him, her gray hair at the level of his chin. "The funeral isn't for Syd. He knows that. Funerals aren't for the dead. They're for the living. That's a coldhearted, bitter thing for him to do, goddamn it. He's a bastard and he hasn't got the right!"

"It was his life," Gramps says.

"Not anymore it isn't!"

I'm surprised by Grandma. What she's said strikes me as particularly wise, a wisdom I don't credit her with nearly enough. We all attribute wisdom to Gramps because he's so quiet, and we equate Grandma's chatter with superficiality, when perhaps the ratio of words spoken to folly or wisdom indicates nothing but habit, predisposition. But more than this, I'm taken by my grandmother's fierceness, by her absolute loyalty, and by her insight into Gramps's emotional core. Gramps wants to say good-bye to his only brother, whom he looked up to his entire childhood and most of his life, and Syd has taken that from him, a deliberate and unforgivable act of cruelty.

Grandma says, "It's a good thing he's dead, or I'd go up there and kill him myself." She's simmering down, but she's serious, and she's flustered by the smiles on all our faces, on everyone's face but Gramps's. "You think I'm joking, but I'm not."

"No, Grandma," Mel says. "We know you're not."

"Then what's so funny?"

"Nothing. Not a thing."

"The bastard has no right to do that to his family."

"No, he doesn't. Not at all."

"Goddamn right."

Gramps doesn't go home at noon, and neither does Grandma. I fix some vegetable beef soup for lunch, and the three of us eat at the kitchen table in the back of the store. Gramps doesn't say a word. Grandma and I talk about Syd, about how, after the Tremewans lost the ranch, he left Nevada and worked the rest of his life in Boise as a machinist, about how he never was the same after his wife, Adelaide, died, like a switch had been flipped inside his brain. Gramps isn't listening. He takes the broom and dustpan and goes out and sweeps the aisles, something we usually don't do on Saturday because it's so busy. But it's one of the few things he still can do. He can't make out price stickers or the small keys on the cash register, so he can't stock shelves or wait on customers. He can bag groceries, so that's what he does most often.

Later in the day, Gramps bags groceries for Mel, and when the store is empty, he sits up on the counter. He still hasn't said anything about Syd, but his face has loosened, its stiff musculature gone.

"You remember old Pete Roa, don't you, Gramps?" Mel asks.

Gramps nods his head.

"You remember how when Pete got cancer, he was off in Salt Lake for what seemed like a year, going through all the treatments?"

Gramps nods again.

"Well, after he came back, he came in the store here to talk to me.

"'Mel,' he said, 'I don't know how much longer I got, so I figured I ought to come in and pay my bill.'

" 'I appreciate that, Pete, I really do,' I said. 'And you know, you don't look half bad. I've seen a lot worse. Looks like you might ride out the month even.'

" 'Maybe I will.'

" 'I'd give you three weeks, easy.'

" 'You're a real peach, Mel. A hell of a guy.'

" 'I know it. I'm here for you.'

" 'I'll tell you one problem I got. I don't know what to do with the money I've saved up. I can't stand my ex-wife, or my son. I got a few deadbeat nephews I don't care much for.'

" 'I'll tell you what, Pete. I'll write you out a check for what you're worth. You give me the cash, and I'll bury you with the check. How does that sound?'

" 'You'd like that, wouldn't you, Basco?'

" 'Yes I would.'

" 'But you can't take it with you.'

" 'Now, Pete, that's true, and it isn't.'

" 'How's that?'

" 'You can't take *your* money with you. But you can sure as hell take *mine*. I've had plenty of folks do that over the years. Wonderful credit system we have here. It's got a few loopholes, and that's one. Which is why I'm sure glad to see you today, Pete. I'm not too religious, but I've been praying for you, hoping you'd hang on long enough to come in here and pay your bill. You owe me plenty.' "

Mel takes a step back, looks around. He has a gift, an artist's gift, and it has to do with storytelling, with creating a certain kind of atmosphere. He knows how and when to use this gift, and he just has, bringing an old itinerant miner back from the dead and placing him in a context where he could be of help to Gramps, a help that anyone around here would want to give him but might not know how to do. Gramps is smiling, and his mind, for the moment, is off of his brother and his own hurt, and this is what Mel was after, and only this, and now it's over and the day can go on.

Nov 5, 1997

Dear Greg:

so happy to hear from you. Yes the snow is over a foot out
our back door and its below the ought and yes oliver is still
wearing his green sweatshirt and walking to the store every
morning—

We have a couple in apartment 1 with 2 cats no less and a
man in apartment 4—lives in carlin during the week and here
over the weekend but it pays the propane bill so thats all right.
It snowed for 2 days. I didn't have you to clean the snow off the
walk to court—had to do it myself and it is still snowing—
Monday Dick Prunty shot himself with a 22—I guess the
funeral will be friday. Their all snowed in in Charleston.

Eddie says he misses you at the Miners in the mornings. No
one to play anymore. Dorothy had to have surgery again on her
Spine. you know she had surgery on her spine in September—
had a tumor on her spine.

Glad you liked Mexico. We never did get to see any of the
Missions when we were there—guess now we never will—
Well I must close now and get this in the mail

Love you

grandma and grandpa T

Christmas Eve. Everybody from town is gathered down on the road shoulder by the Volunteer Fire Department. A bonfire's going in the hubcap of an old tractor wheel, and Colon has turned on the flashing lights of his state trooper to make sure motorists passing through town go especially slow. Inside the firehouse, there's a table with homemade cookies and fruitcake and the coffee machine from Tremewan's Store full of hot chocolate. Bobbie Culley hands out weathered copies of *A Mountain City Christmas,* and we all sing carols. The stars above the mountains are cold and distant, and everybody's bundled up and stamping their feet to keep warm. Most of the old-timers are wearing their snowmobile suits and moon boots, as if any minute they might sled down the hill into the meadow. Mel passes around a bottle of amaretto to liven up the hot chocolate and loosen the vocal cords.

We've just sung "Away in a Manger," and Mel says to Jim Connolley, "It's amazing the words they get you to say in these

Christmas songs. You're not going to find them all in the dictionary. Take *lowing,* for example. The cattle are *lowing?*"

"My cows don't low," Jim says.

"Here's another thing," Mel says. "I've thought about this, but I don't think there's a way in a manger, not with all them animals around."

"How about a hayloft?" Jim says.

"Now that's been done," Mel says.

Mel applies this sort of scrutiny to each song. It's not hard to imagine what he must have been like as a kid in the church choir.

At midnight, everybody's feeling pretty cheery, and we plug in the Mountain City Christmas tree, sing "Silent Night," and then everybody goes home to bed.

Christmas night. We're driving back to Mountain City from Elko after spending the day with family at Aunt Sarah and Uncle George's. Gramps is in the passenger seat, Grandma's in the back, and I'm driving. I can hardly see the road. Snow drifts across the asphalt like fog, rising sometimes an inch off the road surface, sometimes a foot. If I look hard, training my eyes, I can usually make out the yellow lines of the center lane, or the solid white line of the road's edge. I've been driving twenty miles an hour. Sometimes the wind picks up, and out the windshield the pale beams of the headlights illuminate nothing but white. Flurries everywhere, obscuring everything. I see what Gramps sees. Shadows. Suggestions of the physical world. I stop the car and wait. I have the heater going, and the inside of the car is warm and comfortable. I've stopped several times. Embankments on either side of the highway sometimes drop off ten or fifteen feet. Twenty years ago, my cousin Raymond, Mel and Lou's third son, was killed in a car accident on this highway somewhere near here. He was sixteen. He is on my mind now, and he is probably on the minds of Grandma and Gramps also, though none of us says anything. We are always quiet on this stretch of the highway.

This morning, when we left Mountain City for Elko, Grandma forgot to bring Gramps's medicine bag. If she hadn't, we'd still be at Sarah's, waiting out the storm. Grandma's been forgetting a lot of things lately. The small leather bag is sitting now on the table in the kitchen, and it contains the host of pills that help keep Gramps alive. He's already missed one round of medications. If I can keep us on the road, if we don't get rear-ended or hit head on, he won't miss another.

Two weeks after Thanksgiving, Gramps suffered a stroke. Blood vessels burst in the cavity behind his eyes, hemorrhaging for over an hour before the pain and nausea grew so severe that Gramps complained. He stayed in the hospital in Elko for five days. His doctor believed it was his first stroke, or at least his first major stroke. There was a possibility that he'd been suffering small, minor strokes for some time. Fortunately, he suffered no permanent damage, no paralysis or loss of mental ability. Afterwards, he even seemed relieved, as if he'd come to some measure of acceptance. When he sat in his chair at night listening to the television, to the news or a ball game, he didn't wring his hands or clench the chair's arms. He held his hands in his lap. Sometimes he pulled his quilt up to his neck and dozed off.

During his stay in the hospital, he'd made a living will. He wanted no extraordinary measures to keep him alive. But his doctor had given him pills to take, to go along with all the other pills he already took, and he needed to take them three times a day.

In the eighty-four miles from Elko to Mountain City, there are no towns and few people. A handful of people. The land is wide open, a long valley running north and south between hills and mountains. Ranch land. More than twenty ranches are spread out to the east and west of Highway 225, which cuts the valley in two. The old Tremewan Ranch is on the north fork of the Humboldt River, roughly halfway between Elko and Mountain City, on the west side of the road. It has changed hands many times since Gramps and his dad lost it to the Depression. Now it's called the Triple Creek Ranch. Gramps has walked or ridden or driven over almost every inch of this valley. He knows it, and the road that passes through it, the road we're traveling on now, by instinct, the same way he once knew how to see.

I was eight years old when my cousin Raymond died in a car accident on the Mountain City highway. It was a Friday afternoon, and he was traveling home to Mountain City from Elko, where he and my cousin Molly went to high school, where they lived during the week at my aunt Sarah's. Raymond and Molly were in the backseat of the car. The woman driving lost control and the car rolled. She doesn't remember why or how. She lived. Molly broke her back, but she lived. Ellen

Thompson, Norman's wife, was in the car also, in the passenger seat, and she was holding in her lap a six-month-old infant, the driver's daughter. The baby lived. Ellen died, the little girl cradled in her arms.

I was asleep upstairs in our house in Lincoln, Nebraska, where we were living then, and I didn't hear the phone ring. What I woke to was a sound I couldn't comprehend. It was perhaps the strangest, most eerie sound I have ever heard. It was my mother's wailing. I went downstairs and stood beside her quietly, the way any child would, wanting to do something, anything, to make her stop, but not having any idea how to do that. Still holding the phone and screaming now, my mother pulled me to herself, my head between her rib cage and forearm, and she squeezed, too hard, so that it hurt, so that in almost any other context it would have been wrong, but it wasn't, not then. She was making sure I was alive.

We left that morning for Nevada and the funeral, and there is very little that I remember about that time. I remember watching my uncle Mel, his head in his hands, and my aunt Lou in a black dress with a veil over her face. They were sitting outside in the first of several rows of chairs. It was a clear, sunny day. Others must have been beside them or behind them, and I think there may have been a canopy too, or a tent of some kind, like the kind I have seen at other funerals in my life. There must have been a casket also and a hole in the ground, but I don't remember any of those things. I do remember that I had heard from someone that my uncle Mel had had to go into the basement of some building and identify the body. I am tempted to think that I wondered what he must have said then, like "Yes" or "No" or

"Raymond" or "My boy's gone." But that isn't possible, that wondering. I was only eight years old and was as blind to those things as the wind.

"Them's the lights of the PX," Gramps says. "You've got thirty miles."

I'd seen the lights coming closer for some time, and I had guessed they were the maintenance station or the PX, but I wasn't sure. Gramps can't tell a man from a woman from twenty feet away, but he could see those lights. He must have known where the road curved or dipped or rose and then added that to the flicker out the corners of his eyes, the change from a darker to a lighter gray. He knows exactly where we are.

Grandma says, "Oliver, should we stop at the PX and call Lou?" Grandma's voice is calm. She was worried before, we were all worried, but a relief has come over us with the ranch's glimmer in the distance, like a lighthouse beam through a sea of snow.

"No need, Anna," Gramps says, turning to her from the front seat so that she can see his lips. "Greg's doing a good job. He'll get us home."

"Okay, dear," Grandma says. And then she taps me hard on the shoulder and says, "You know, he never says that about *my* driving."

Then we're all grinning. It's true. Gramps rarely says anything good about Grandma's driving, even though she rarely drives more than the quarter mile between home and the store. For years and years, Grandma never drove. When she and Gramps went anywhere, he always drove. When she went to Elko or

Boise with Lou, Lou drove. And then one day as Gramps drove Mel up to the house from the store, Mel could see him listening for the sound of the tires on the edge of the gravel shoulder. I don't know what Mel said to him then, but he said something. Gramps never drove again.

Since then, when it's just the two of them, Grandma does all the driving, with Gramps grumbling beside her, giving her directions, frustrated that he can no longer do something so simple as drive.

The ranch lights are brighter now, unmistakable, and Gramps says, still turned and looking back, "You're getting better every day, Grandma."

"I get us there, don't I?" Grandma says.

"Yes," Gramps says. "You do."

Then I realize I'm happy. I'm happy to be in a blizzard with my grandparents, sharing this time with them as their health fades and they enter their last days, however graceful or awkward. It's instructive, these things they say to each other, in teasing, in love, after sixty-two years of marriage. They're teaching me how to grow old.

When we drop down into the canyon, the frozen cliff walls rise up to block the storm, and I can see the road clearly as it winds beside the black Owyhee. After sixteen slow miles, the canyon opens again on the wind, and in the distance glows Mountain City.

In the last few days of December the weather warms, and in the afternoons snow melts from roofs and runs down gutters and drips from eaves. At night the temperature plummets, and by morning ice collects in the gravel and spreads itself thin over steps and porches and the highway. These mornings, I drive Gramps down to the store.

Before breakfast, I go out to the garage, start the engine of the car, and turn the heater on. After breakfast, when we walk from the house to the garage, I hold Gramps's arm firmly to steady him over the ice, to catch him if he loses his balance. He walks deliberately, like a man fording a river, the current strong at his knees, the stones slippery. Like an old man fording a river. At times, I grip his arm so tightly I cause a bruise. He bruises easily. He never says anything. At night I see the purple cloud of blood on his upper arm beneath the undershirt he wears to bed.

Later that winter, my uncle George carves Gramps a cane. Like most canes, it has a round rubber shoe on its bottom and a smooth, curved handle. Below the curve, George has engraved the bust of a mustang, the details so intricately rendered that it must have taken him days to finish. George wants Gramps to *see* the horse with his fingers. The horse's neck arched and rearing back, its eyes rolling wildly, its nostrils flared. Gramps has always refused to use a cane before, and so George makes him one he has to use, or else seem ungrateful. George is banking on that. The cane's craftsmanship is also, in another way, a credit to George's consideration. People lavish attention on the cane, on how well it was made, and not on the fact that Gramps now has to use one. George has been around too many old cowboys not to know a few things about pride.

February 4, 1998

Happy Birthday Greg: I guess you have settled down to the old grind again. We miss you. Cowboy Poetry time—you should have been here to tell a few poems. Ha. We never went—I cant hear and gramps cant see so thats the way it goes.

What do you think of your mom and Di and Graham going to the Basque Country? I think its great—wish I could go too but I cant leave Oliver for 3 weeks and he doesnt want to go— been once he said. Have a good day.

Love you

grandma and grandpa T

When Mel's jokes are crass, he warns his audience. "This one here's got a little edge to it. Don't tell it at dinner over at the minister's."

An old couple from Missouri drives out to Nevada to play the slots in Reno, see the casinos. They stop to get gas in Winnemucca. Full service. Now the old lady's going deaf—kind of like one Basco lady I know here in town—and the attendant comes over and asks the old fella if he wants to fill her up, and the old fella says yes.

"What did he say?" (Mel's cupping his hand to his ear.)

"He asked if he should fill her up and I told him yes." (Mel mouths out each word exaggeratedly.)

Pretty soon the attendant comes back and asks the old guy if he wants his oil checked, and the old guy says yes, he does.

"What did he say?"

"He asked if I wanted the oil checked and I told him yes, I do."

So the attendant checks the oil and comes back and says, "Say, mister, I noticed you folks was from Missouri." And then the attendant leans forward and says a little quieter to the old man, "You know, I been there once. Pretty good place. But you know what?"

"What's that?"

"The worst piece of ass I ever had was in Missouri."

The old guy smiles and puts the car in gear, waves to the attendant, and drives off.

"What did he say?"

"He says he knows you."

March 20, 1998

Dear Gregory

We're doing fine Oliver is doing real good. I broke a tooth Tuesday on some Hard Candy and I know better.

Love for now

grandma and grandpa T

Hope you can read this my writing gets worse

Grandma is in the bathroom. She's been in there forty-five minutes. She hasn't showered or bathed, and my mom can't figure out what's taking her so long. Mom can hear her moving around, making noise, so she knows Grandma's okay. But what's she doing?

My mom came to Mountain City from the East Coast a few days before. She came to visit, and to help Gramps retire from his judgeship.

For the past couple of years, since Gramps's vision started going, Grandma has acted as his clerk. She's read his correspondence to him, taken notes during court, typed up all the documents to be sent to Elko. It's been a true partnership, good for both of them, keeping them sharp, active.

But Grandma can't do those things anymore. Her hearing is shot all to hell, the ringing in her ears like the fading reverberations of a rifle blast, an aftermath without beginning or end. Hearing aids don't help. She can't hear testimonies in court. She can't hear Gramps's dictations unless he shouts, which tires him, tears at the muscles in his throat. Finally, one night at dinner, Gramps interrupted Lou's shouting at Grandma about their upcoming quilting meeting.

"I can't do the judgeship," Gramps said. "I'm going to resign. Somebody else has got to do it now." Then he got up and went to sit in his chair in the living room.

"*What* did he say?" Grandma said. "*What's* he so upset about?"

There were other options. Gramps could hire a clerk. There wasn't anyone in Mountain City with the time, inclination, and ability to do the job, but the county was willing to pay for a clerk to travel to Mountain City on the days court was in session. Gramps wouldn't hear of it. He still wanted to be the justice of the peace, but he didn't want to do the job without Grandma. He couldn't do it by himself, and he wouldn't do it without her.

After that, Grandma stayed quiet for days, hardly talking to anyone, feeling sorry for herself. "I'm no good anymore. I know that," she'd say.

My mom hadn't seen Grandma in four months, and she knew that something had changed, worsened, since the last time she'd visited, something more than hearing loss. She saw how listless, how inattentive, Grandma had become at the dinner table, how Grandma's eyes tracked along the far wall unless she was spoken to directly. Grandma said she'd been having dreadful headaches. She only said so because someone finally asked. "How have you been feeling lately, Mom? Have you been sleeping well? Headaches? Anything?"

"Well, yes, now that you say so. I have had these terrible headaches."

"For how long?"

"Oh, quite a long time."

When Mom asked why she hadn't said anything earlier, Grandma said she didn't want to "cry wolf."

John Henry, the Idaho Power man, came into the store and asked Lou if Grandma had been well lately.

"Just fine. Why do you ask?"

"Well, it's just that she hasn't paid her bill now for quite a long time. Now, Lou, you know I'd never turn their power off, but I thought I'd come in and say something."

Mom and Lou went through Grandma's checkbook. It hadn't been balanced for months. The checks were listed like prime numbers, the gaps of attention like collapsed synapses. It had never been like this. Grandma had always been thoroughly capable, excellent even, with figures. Before she retired, she had kept the store's books for twenty years. But she hadn't cashed their last three Social Security checks. They found them in a drawer with some old clipped coupons for the new Wal-Mart in Elko.

That night at dinner Mom asked Gramps if he'd noticed anything like this before. She asked the question with Grandma sitting right there, like she was a child and couldn't understand "grown-up talk." Gramps said yes, he had noticed a few things. Once he'd seen her sit at the kitchen table with the checkbook open for hours, but he never saw her write a check, never saw her pick up a pen.

"Why didn't you say anything?" my mom said, raising her voice, which Grandma heard.

"Say *what?*" Grandma asked. "*What* didn't he say?"

Gramps didn't answer.

Mom and Lou balanced the checkbook, paid bills, and cashed checks. They filled out the paperwork, made phone calls, and retired Gramps from his judgeship. In the evenings, they talked about senility, about taking Grandma to see a doctor for her headaches.

Grandma's been in the bathroom over an hour. Mom knocks loudly on the door. "What are you doing in there? Can I come in?"

"Dolores," Grandma says, like she expected her just then, like she was waiting the whole time, "could you help me with this, here? I've been trying and trying and I can't figure it. I know I should know how, but I don't for some reason."

Grandma can't get her bra on.

The next day Lou and my mom take Grandma to the hospital in Boise.

On her way back to Mountain City from the hospital in Boise, Grandma asked Lou and my mom to stop at the Target so she could buy a new pair of shoes. "Tennies," she called them. "I need to get some tennies," she said, like she was still a little girl and not an eighty-four-year-old great-grandmother who had just been diagnosed with a lung cancer that had spread to her brain. She had a tumor the size of a child's fist in her brain. The doctor said she had two months, at the most, to live. My mom and Lou didn't want to stop at the Target. They wanted to drive their grief the 180 miles through the Bruneau desert, across the emptiness of the reservation, and into the canyon beside the Owyhee. They wanted to go home. But Grandma insisted. So they went to the Target, and Grandma bought her tennies. Keds. White, canvas, rubber-soled, nondescript shoes. Twelve-dollar shoes. Her pair at home had worn out, she said. The shoe box went into a bag and was later put in Grandma's closet at home. She never wore them. My grandmother was an optimist. She could be moody and unpredictable, depressed at times, like most people, but at the bottom, beneath all that, she was an optimist, which is not the same as being hopeful or possessing faith, and it is not a neglect or refusal of fact; it is something entirely different.

After Grandma came home from the hospital, and people started coming by the house to visit—Rosella, Bobbie, Margaret, Dorothy, Eddie, relatives from all over Elko County—Grandma told them, "It's funny that it's lung cancer, cause I never smoked. Lenore smoked and she got it, lung cancer. The doctor says there's a tumor. I never did think there was anything up there, but I guess there was." Understated, matter of fact, joking, Grandma told everyone of her condition. She made no bold proclamations. She wasn't going to change anything. She did have my cousin Mitch go up to court and bring a typewriter down to the house. Her penmanship was no good anymore, and she intended to type all her letters from then on. The dutiful fetching of the typewriter probably would have been my job, had I been living there then, and I like to think now that she meant to write me first. But she never wrote another letter, never took the dustcover off the keyboard. That doesn't matter. Grandma was an optimist. How you feel about living in the world is who you are.

Gramps stopped going down to the store in the mornings so he could be with Grandma whenever she was awake. She'd undergone minor radiation treatments at the hospital in Boise to reduce the tumor's pressure, to relieve the sharp headaches she'd been having for months. She stayed in bed most of the time, and

Gramps sat beside her for hours in a hard, ladder-back chair. Her condition deteriorated rapidly, at a rate that seemed surreal. Something about the medicine she was taking caused her face to swell, leaving her looking bloated and different. Gramps broke out in hives, red dots all over his chest, his back, the undersides of his arms. A man came from the medical supply store in Elko and set up a hospital bed for Grandma beside the bed Gramps would from then on sleep in alone.

All four Tremewan daughters gathered around Grandma and Gramps: my mother stayed on in Mountain City; Sarah came every day from Elko; Di came from Cedar City with Graham; Lou spent more time up at the house than down at the store.

Grandma rarely left her hospital bed. Mom and Di and Sarah and Lou took turns at all the things that needed to be done. They changed Grandma's bedpans and soiled linens. They gave her sponge baths. They massaged the stiff, knotted muscles in her shoulders and back.

Sometimes Graham sat in the chair beside Grandma. He held her hand. Sometimes he said, "Sky West *is* going to Salt Lake. It *is*." He insisted. Sometimes he said, "*Grandma* is dying." Grandma couldn't hear a word, but when her mind was clear, she'd smile and say, "*Who* flew the plane to Salt Lake?" And Graham would answer, "*I* did. *I* flew the plane to Salt Lake," and he would laugh and pat Grandma's hand with his, and Grandma would be asleep again. She spoke less and less.

Grandma did not want to eat. She had to be fed, one spoonful at a time, with considerable coaxing and encouragement. She slept through family dinners. One night, after everyone at the table had lapsed into silence, Lou broke the quiet sharply, shaking her finger at Gramps. "Don't think that because Grandma's going to die that you can die too." Then it was quiet again. And then Gramps said, to no one, staring down at his pie plate, "I'm not going anywhere. After this is all over, I'm staying right here."

Less than three weeks after coming home from the hospital, Grandma died in her sleep. It was the middle of the afternoon. Rosella had been to see her only an hour or so before. Rosella had come every day, a fact which, though not surprising, is as important to me now as any fact I know. Sarah came in with Grandma's three o'clock medication. Then Mom and Lou and Sarah and Di and Graham stood around Grandma. Gramps sat in his chair, his hands in his lap. Lou phoned down to the store to tell Mel. Mel couldn't come up to the house. He couldn't. When Colon came to the house to act as coroner, Gramps met him at the door. Colon put his hand on Gramps's shoulder and said, "I'm sorry, Oliver." Gramps nodded and said, "She's in there," and he went back and sat in his chair. Colon pronounced Grandma dead, and then the ambulance came from the hospital in Owyhee and took Grandma to Elko.

At Grandma's wake, the priest showed up an hour late, and so my mom and dad went up to the lectern and led us all in the rosary. Most of us didn't know how to work our rosaries, but that didn't matter because it's what Grandma would have wanted. I sat next to my great-aunt Ayah, Grandma's twin, who lived in Denver and who was now the last Zabala. She took me by the hand and whispered that this was just like when she and Anna were little, in the recyvydor at the Overland, and I wasn't prepared to hear that then.

The next morning, Graham and I and our cousins were pall-
bearers and Graham kept saying, "*Grandma's* dead. She died. Yes
she *did*," and one of us would say, "That's right, Graham.
Grandma *is* dead. It's very sad," and we didn't know what we
were saying.

I had never seen my grandfather cry before that morning.
He sobbed and sobbed. It didn't look like he was capable of
stopping. I cried too, but for some reason I couldn't cry for
Grandma, not yet. The tears just wouldn't come. But I would
look at Gramps, and I could cry for him. I never believed, I
hadn't even contemplated the possibility of Grandma dying
before Gramps. I don't know that I can contemplate it now. We
always worried over Gramps, never Grandma. Sometimes she
said she thought she was being "taken for granite," and she was.
She was supposed to be the rock, the sturdy one.

It's almost June, and in Mountain City, only Jim Connolley wakes each day to darkness, which for him has as much to do with principle as it does with cows. Gramps walks in the front door of Tremewan's Store. The lights aren't on yet in the front, and the dimness accentuates the electric blue light from the soda case and produce bins. He sits up on one of the counters. His feet dangle, like always, above the floor, but now his boots are untied, loose, the laces hanging limp. He doesn't need to see to tie his shoes. That's not what he needs. He just has difficulty bending that far. Grandma used to tie them.

Mel comes up the main aisle from the back, moves over beside Gramps, and again, like every morning this month, wraps his arms around this man he loves so much, lets his hands stray across his back and shoulders. Then he kneels down and ties Gramps's boots, vigorously, jerking the strips of leather through the grommets, pulling one leg and then the other forward against his chest.

"I used to be able to tie them sonsabitches," Gramps says.

Mel nods his head and says nothing.

Less than a month after Grandma died, Gramps found out that both of his remaining sisters have cancer. Ruth and Lucille. And now Rosella's slipping again. Today, Lee came in the store, his face burning red, simmering, matching his hair.

"You folks got to stop selling my mom carrots," he said angrily. "We've got more up there than you've got down here."

"Return them. We'll take them back," Lou said without looking up, her voice traveling down and through the credit book she was studying, a pencil in her hand.

"I don't care about that," Lee said.

"What is it then?"

"You know what it is. She buys the same things two and three times a day. She forgets she has a list in her pocket. Then she finds the list and buys them a fourth time."

Lou looked up from her figures.

"You want us to put up a sign, Lee? Is that it? We know. We're trying. But it's not always the same one of us up here running the registers. We can't do any more than we're doing. If you won't return them, feed the goddamn carrots to the jackrabbits."

"Don't get sore at me, Lou. I'm not saying it's your fault."

"It's nobody's fault, Lee. But that doesn't mean I can't cuss somebody out too, same as you, and you're standing there. You'll do just fine."

"Okay. Okay. Just watch out for the carrots, please. That's all I'm saying."

"Watch out yourself."

The other day a homesick Peruvian shepherd jammed thirty dollars' worth of quarters in the phone booth on the front porch of Tremewan's Store. Mel had to go out and empty the change box so he could keep calling. As the coins poured into the gunnysack in Mel's hands, the two men exchanged nods. The herder wore jeans and a jean jacket and worn leather boots. Beard stubble shadowed his cheeks and jaw. A blue heeler lay curled at his feet, waiting, entirely obedient. There haven't been Basque sheepherders in northern Nevada for nearly thirty years. They're all from South America now, Chileans, Peruvians. Mel said later it was like that Peruvian had stepped out from the pages of one of Grandma's Basco coffee table books. He said it was hard to see him in color.

At dinnertime I come in from playing down in the meadow by the river. I wash up and go to Grandma for inspection. Am I clean enough? That is always the question. I am rarely clean enough. Sometimes Grandma takes hold of my wrists, pulls my arms above my head, and twists them each a little, so that I see the offense for myself. Elbows. Dirty, dried-up, dead-skinned elbows.

"Ahuntzen belaunkoskorrak! Look at them. Do you see them? See for yourself. *Ahuntzen belaunkoskorrak!"* She tugs and twists my skin, like it's elastic, rubber. "Wash up and come back to me."

Ahuntzen belaunkoskorrak! means "Goat's knees!" My elbows are like the knees of goats.

Gramps is the only widower in Mountain City.

I dreamt I visited my aunt Lou in the hospital in Owyhee, which was strange because Lou, like Grandma, had never been sick before that I knew of. I was sitting beside her and she was lying in her hospital bed and she had the covers tucked under her chin, like a little girl, and her fingers were curled over the hem of the top cover, like a little girl, and the top cover was the quilt that Grandma had made for me when I was born, red barns on a creamy white background, like the barns were flying through the clouds. Lou's little girl fingers were so thin, the skin translucent, the bone visible, like in X rays, and she was so old, her hair brittle, like ryegrass after the first frost. She kept asking me where her mom and dad were, and I kept saying we didn't call them that, that we all said *Grandma* and *Gramps,* and Grandma and Gramps were back in Mountain City at the store, waiting on customers like the old days, holding down the fort. Then she asked me where she was, and I told her the hospital on the reservation. She wanted to know why, and I told her pneumonia, that she had pneumonia, and I said it twice like that, like Grandma would have. Then Lou said she didn't know anything about that, pneumonia. She wanted to know why no one had told her. I told her I was waiting for the right moment, and I wanted to tell her now.

Since Grandma died, Gramps pours his own milk. He takes a small plastic glass from the cupboard and sets it on the counter. He finds the milk on the left side of the top shelf of the refrigerator. Two percent, plastic half gallon, with a handle. He sets it down near the glass and unscrews the lid. With his left hand, he lifts the glass. With his right, the milk. He raises both up to the level of his face. Inches from his face. Like a chemist with a laboratory flask. He angles the container and the milk cascades past him. He looks away from the falling milk toward the window so he can glimpse the process in motion, peripherally, the only way he can. The blind can pour milk. He knows that. But he's not blind, not yet, and so their method can wait, whatever it is. He sets the filled glass down on the kitchen table, pats the counter for the lid, screws it back on, and returns the half gallon to where it belongs. The glass rests now beside a small plastic bowl on a place mat at the table. In the bowl are several pills, including Coumadin, a thinner, which helps his blood flow skyward, against gravity, to his brain.

Zer esan, Amama? What do you say, Grandma?
Esan ezer ez. I say nothing.

In the fall of 1919, Oliver went with Syd and his father to ship the cattle at the railroad at Deeth. On their return, they stopped in Elko, bought the groceries and supplies that would last them through the next year, and hauled them home in the back of their wagon. They were gone five days. Oliver had never been to Deeth or to Elko, but that didn't matter to him now.

They stored the food beneath their homestead in the cellar, where it was cool, or cold, in every season, and dry. They stored hundred-pound sacks of flour and sugar. A fifty-gallon barrel of coffee beans. Canned tomatoes and string beans and corn from the garden. They buried the garden's carrots and cabbages and turnips and potatoes deep in sand, so that Oliver had to stick his arm in to the shoulder and rummage around. On the smoothed dirt floor were pans of milk and butter, covered with dish towels. A twenty-five-pound box of dried fruit from which Edith made pies. Edith had turned twelve, and her dad and two brothers and two sisters loved pies.

School began. In Nevada then, in rural areas, the state supported a school district if three children attended. For four years, until Oliver grew old enough to join Syd and Edith, the Tremewans had provided room and board to a teacher with a school-age child. Now, Oliver was old enough, and his aunt Lila, his father's sister, had come late that summer to live with them, and she ran the school that stood alongside their homestead. The school's wood floor measured eight by twelve feet, and over this, a white canvas tent provided sidewalls and roof. In the small space Oliver struggled daily to keep still. He felt cooped up, awkward, when just outside, the world stretched away without boundaries of any kind.

Winter came, and when the schoolday ended, Oliver took his dog, Turk, a yellow Australian shepherd his father had brought back from Elko that fall, and together they scouted the immediate perimeter of the ranch for coyotes. With his gun strapped over his shoulder, Oliver traveled on white-pine skis that Syd had made for him from trees high up in the Independence. Returning at dusk he heard the coyotes' eerie yipping in the gray distance. When there were no coyotes, he shot rabbits. The rabbits fed on and in the bottoms of the haystacks, and Oliver sent Turk burrowing after them, scattering them over the white meadow in a hundred directions. Sometimes the Tremewans would eat rabbit for supper. Sometimes, after dark, the rabbits clustered silently at the edges of the yard. They stood upright on their back legs and bared their pale chests and throats. They seemed frozen. Their rabbit eyes glowed dimly above the sheen of moonlit snow. On the porch Turk growled low and whined. Then Oliver would go inside.

In June, each morning after Oliver finished with the milk

cows and chickens and pigs and lambs, he and Turk went down to the north fork of the Humboldt River. He carried fishing line, and with his pocketknife he'd cut a willow branch and fish for trout for a few hours.

That summer, the Tremewans did not go to Mountain City for the Fourth of July.

Last week, Lee took Rosella to Elko and put her in the nursing home. He couldn't afford to quit his job at the mine and look after her full-time. He'd come home late one night from work and found her out kneeling in the garden. A million stars shone above them. Rosella hadn't worked in the garden in years. She didn't recognize him at first. She was cold. When he picked her up to carry her inside, every bit of her—her hair, her clothes, the open palm she put to his cheek—smelled like sagebrush.

Home means different things to different people. Rosella lived in Mountain City for sixty years. I wasn't raised in Mountain City, I don't live there now, and I'll never live there again. I visit every few months. To me, *home* is the place I can't keep from disappearing. Rosella. Grandma. Thirty-one people live in Mountain City.

Sometimes, as Gramps makes his way from the kitchen to the living room, his oxygen cord gets snagged by the tiny metal foot on the bottom corner of the refrigerator, and when the cord plays out, it tugs at his ears and jerks his head like a roped calf.

Sometimes after Gramps goes to bed, I'll be watching TV when I hear a wild, calamitous beeping, like a sixteen-wheeler is backing into the living room. It's Gramps's oxygen machine, indicating that the flow of air is somehow being blocked. The cord, running beneath the closed door to Gramps's bedroom, is crimped. Sometimes he opens the door, rearranges the cord, and the beeping stops. Sometimes I do it for him, looking in on him quickly while he's sleeping, checking, making sure, trying to stay calm.

Sometimes I come through the front door of the store after getting the mail or running some errand, and Gramps is standing there alone at the front counters whistling to himself or jingling the change in his pockets and staring off into the distances of the store.

A pipe that drains rainwater and snowmelt off the flat roof of the apartments has snapped at the joint where it turns to go down the side of the building. Gramps is tired of it leaking onto the back porch, and so he's got me up on this rickety wooden extension ladder that belongs in a museum. I'm two stories high, praying the wind stays calm, and Gramps is directly below me on the ground, acting like steadying the ladder is possible. I end up rigging what Grandma would have called a Basco lash-up job. Baling twine and duct tape.

"You know this isn't going to last," I shout down at Gramps.

"It's only got to last as long as I do."